Handcrafted
CARDS, BAGS,
BOXES & **TAGS**

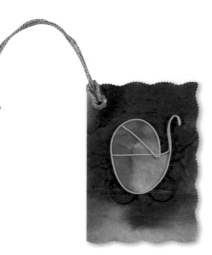

Handcrafted
CARDS, BAGS,
BOXES & **TAGS**

Kate MacFadyen

wirecraft embellishments for all occasions

First published 2006 by
Guild of Master Craftsman Publications Ltd,
166 High Street, Lewes,
East Sussex BN7 1XU

Text © Kate MacFadyen, 2006
Copyright in the Work © Guild of Master Craftsman Publications Ltd, 2006

ISBN 1 86108 467 6
A catalogue record of this book is available from the British Library.

Production Manager: Hilary MacCallum
Managing Editor: Gerrie Purcell
Editor: Rachel Netherwood
Photography: Anthony Bailey
Managing Art Editor: Gilda Pacitti
Design: Green Tangerine

Typefaces: Helvetica, Bauer Bodoni

Colour origination: Altaimage
Printed and bound: Hing Yip Printing Company Limited

Measurements notice
Imperial measurements are conversions from metric; they have been rounded up or down
to the nearest ¼, ½ or whole inch. When following the projects, use either the metric
or the imperial measurements; do not mix units.

I dedicate this book to the girls at Artycrafty for all their help and support over the years of crafting, especially Elisabeth and Jenny for their inspirational ideas.

contents

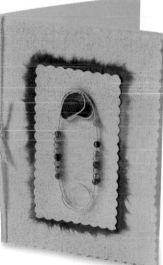

introduction

Having successfully established a method of attaching mulberry paper to a wire frame to create the flowers, butterflies and dragonflies in my first book, Making Wirecraft Cards (2004, GMC Publications), I have further developed this hobby by using the wirecraft in different ways and not just for decorating greeting cards.

These interpretations of nature are delicate but long-lasting if looked after, and well worth the time and effort that you will put into creating them. I hope you will enjoy making these projects, and also that they will inspire you to create your own designs. Have fun!

Wirecraft is an inexpensive and accessible hobby. All materials and equipment used will be available from your local craft shop or by mail order (see page 126 for a list of suppliers).

wirecraft materials and equipment

wires

To make the frames for most of the wirecraft projects in this book you will need 28 gauge (0.3mm) wire. This comes in a variety of colours but the most impressive and user-friendly is copper wire, which is soft and pliable and a real pleasure to work with. Gold and silver wire is less pliable and therefore not quite as easy to work with.

We will also use 34 gauge wire (the higher the number, the thinner the wire) and 21 gauge, plastic-coated wires – all these come in a range of colours including copper, silver and gold.

If you do not want to buy lots of reels in different colours then I suggest getting 28 gauge and 34 gauge wires in copper and silver.

papers

For most of the projects we will use mulberry paper, which comes in a wonderful array of gorgeous colours. It glues well to the wire frame and, because it is thin, the excess paper can be easily trimmed away. I have tried experimenting with tissue and crepe papers, but these are too thin and warp and tear when wet.

On some projects I have used thick, handmade paper and on others I have used angel wire.

This is a very delicate, gauze-like material, with a mesh of fine threads, but just as easy to use as the other papers. All these papers are widely available; you could even have a go at making your own.

beads

There are so many beads available now in different sizes, colours and shapes that you will be spoilt for choice. For the small flower centres you will need small seed beads in assorted colours. For the other projects, such as the butterflies and dragonflies, you will need a selection of beads in different sizes and colours. You will also need accent beads – which are very small beads without holes – for creating 3D flower centres on some of the projects.

adhesive

I have tried many types of glues over the last five years and the glue that still works best for attaching mulberry paper to the wire frame is UHU, an all-purpose glue for metals and plastics. It is stringy in texture and comes in a tube. White PVA and PPA glues are not suitable, because they don't adhere to the wire frame; neither are gel glues because they seem to stay in globules and don't cover the entire frame smoothly.

Buy the smallest tube of UHU you can find because you will need a small nozzle. If you think you can economize by purchasing a large tube that will last a long time, as I did initially, then unfortunately you will find that it not only pours out of the tube the moment you unscrew the lid, but it also thickens with age and is unusable very quickly.

scissors

You will need an old pair of scissors (for cutting the wires) and a pair of embroidery or curved craft scissors (for trimming the mulberry paper away from the wire frame). You will also need an all-purpose pair for cutting the papers and for general use. A decorative pair, for card, bag, tag and box making are not essential, but worthwhile.

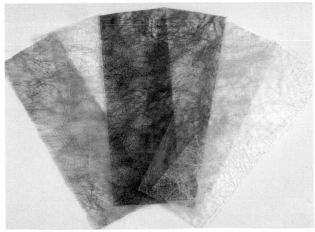

As well as the wirecraft materials, you will need to keep some general equipment and materials in stock for making the cards, boxes, bags and tags.

general materials and equipment

card **is essential for most of the projects. You will need sheets of thin card in white and assorted colours, and thick card for making the sturdier boxes. You can also buy ready-folded cards, which come in various sizes.**

craft knife, ruler and cutting mat **A craft knife is better than scissors for accurately cutting card, as well as the templates for boxes and bags.**

hole punches (plain and decorative) **are useful for adding decorative detail and making the holes for gift bags and tags.**

ribbons **You will need a wide range of ribbons in various widths and colours. Build up a collection of them and keep even the smallest of scraps – they can be used on a tag or a card.**

feathers, bows, sequins **and anything else to decorate your projects that takes your fancy.**

dried flowers **You can pick and dry these yourself (see page 85) or you can buy them already dried and pressed.**

acrylic paints **to decorate the insides of boxes.**

tip

Rummage through second-hand shops and jumble sales for old necklaces that you could dismantle and use for beads.

kitchen towel **You will need this to wipe excess glue from wirecraft frames before attaching mulberry paper.**

tweezers **are brilliant for all craft uses, especially for holding beads and wires.**

round nose pliers **are useful for curling wires, especially the thicker ones.**

cocktail sticks **can be used for curling wires and also for making loops and coils.**

PPA and PVA glues **are ideal for gluing covers to boxes (but not so good for card making as they will crinkle the card).**

double-sided tape **is useful for making all cards, bags and boxes, especially those with glossy surfaces.**

glue dots **for attaching the wirecraft motifs. Using these means that you can reposition the motif if necessary.**

glue sticks **are great for general purpose gluing from cardstock to cardstock (but not for gluing to glossy finishes).**

double-sided foam pads **are useful for creating a 3D raised effect.**

small flower

A small flower is the ideal introduction to the art of wirecraft. Once you have mastered it you will be able to make numerous variations in different shapes and colours.

wirecraft

- **18in (45cm) 28 gauge (0.3mm) copper wire**
- **6in (15cm) 34 gauge (0.2mm) copper wire**
- **12 yellow seed beads**
- **lilac mulberry paper**
- **lilac pastel chalk**
- **cotton bud**

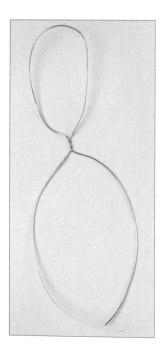

1 Take the 18in (45cm) length of 28 gauge (0.3mm) wire. Find the centre of the wire and form a loop with a 1¼in (3cm) diameter by crossing the wire over itself. Hold the join between your finger and thumb and twist the loop three times, as close to the join as possible. You will now have completed one loop.

2 Working with either the right or left wire, make a second loop twisting the wire as close to the first as possible. You now have two loops.

3 **In the same direction, continue to loop the wire until you have made six petals. There should be two pieces of wire left over. Take these two pieces of wire and twist them together to secure – this then becomes the back of the flower. If you have five or seven petals then you will have made them larger or smaller, but this doesn't matter.**

4 **Using the 6in (15cm) length of 34 gauge (0.2mm) copper wire, wrap one end around the stem to fix in place. Bring the long end of the wire up between two of the petals to the top of the flower (see right).**

5 **Thread three beads onto the wire. Wrap the wire over the centre of the flower, down between two opposite petals and up to the top again. Thread all the beads in this way until there are 12 beads in the centre. This can be fiddly to do because the beads have a tendency to fall down to the back.**

6 **Now it is time to shape the petals. Form a shape by pinching the tip of the petal, then open it out again in the middle (see left). It is important to shape all the petals now, before attaching the paper.**

7 **Cut six pieces (more or less depending on how many petals you have made) of mulberry paper. Make sure each piece is larger than each petal.**

8 **You will have to work quickly through this stage or else the glue will dry before you are ready. Turn the flower over so the back is facing you and have a small piece of paper towel ready. Carefully apply a very thin strip of glue around one petal and immediately remove any excess glue.**

9 **Place a cut piece of mulberry paper to the underside of the glued frame and press gently. Turn the flower over to the right side and trim away the excess paper as close to the framed edge as possible. Glue each petal in turn.**

10 **Trim the wire at the back to about ⅜in (1cm). Use a cotton bud to gently apply lilac-coloured pastel chalk from the centre of the flower to halfway down each petal.**

Christmas

poinsettia

The poinsettia is a beautiful Christmas flower. Once you have learned to adapt the basic flower technique, the poinsettia can be used for all sorts of Christmas projects.

The following technique shows you how to make a poinsettia in traditional red.

tip

The one problem with using red is that it shows the dried glue if you use a lot of it, so take care and practise the technique first.

wirecraft

- 36in (90cm) 28 gauge (0.3mm) red wire
- 6in (15cm) 34 gauge (0.2mm) copper wire
- 14 seed beads in red, green and yellow
- red mulberry paper

1 Take the 36in (90cm) of 28 gauge (0.3mm) red wire and, starting at one end, make four loops that are 1¼in (3cm) long.

2 Keep the wire at the top of the flower then make four more loops that are 1in (2.5cm) long. Make a further four ⅝in (1.5cm) long loops (or three if you haven't enough wire).

3 Secure the wires at the back by twisting them together. This will leave a stem which you can trim off after you have attached the paper to the petals.

4 Attach the 6in (15cm) of 34 gauge (0.2mm) copper wire by wrapping one end around the stem. Bring the long end of the wire up between two petals to the top of the flower.

5 Add four seed beads in yellow. Keeping the seeds on top as much as possible, take the wire down underneath and back up to the top again. Add a few more beads in alternate colours, and continue to wrap them over the centre until you have threaded all the beads.

6 Shape each bract by pinching the tip between your fingers and thumb and gently pulling it open again (see right). Cut 12 pieces of red mulberry paper, larger than each bract.

7 Apply a thin strip of glue to the back of the wire, wipe off the surplus and press the paper onto the glue. Trim away the excess paper close to the framed edge. Glue each petal in turn; you will have to gently move the others up and down and out of the way as you work, to avoid the glue sticking to the other petals. Finally, trim off the stem to about ⅜in (1cm).

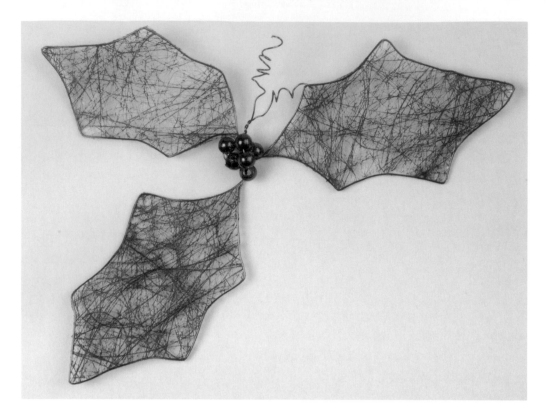

holly

Holly is simple to make and very effective for Christmas decorations. I have made it in a variety of sizes and colours over the years, and if well looked after it will last from one year to the next. You could build up the number of flowers and leaves over the years for decoration from season to season.

wirecraft

- 18in (45cm) 28 gauge (0.3mm) green wire
- 6in (15cm) 34 gauge (0.2mm) copper wire
- 12 red seed beads
- green angel wire

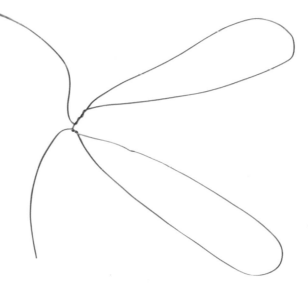

1 Using the 18in (45cm) length of 28 gauge (0.3mm) green wire, make a 2in (5cm) long loop and twist the two wires together.

2 With either the left or right wire, form a second loop, leaving about 1in (2.5cm) of the wire spare and repeat on the other side. You should now have three long loops. Twist the two 1in (2.5cm) spare wires together to secure.

3 Take the 6in (15cm) length of 34 gauge (0.2mm) copper wire and attach the end of it to the short stem. Thread the red beads and wrap them around and between the three loops to make the berries. Wrap the spare wire around the stem to secure.

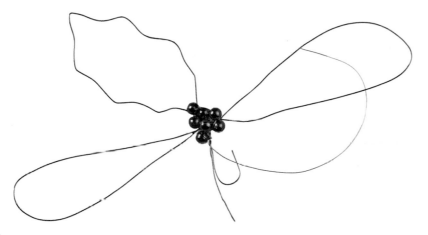

4 To shape the holly leaves, take one of the loops, pinch the point and then three times down each side. It may help you to practise on a spare piece of wire first. Repeat on the other two loops.

5 Cut three pieces of angel wire, slightly larger than the wire leaves. Apply a thin strip of glue to the back of the wire and press the paper onto the glue. Trim away the excess paper close to the framed edge. Glue the leaves one by one.

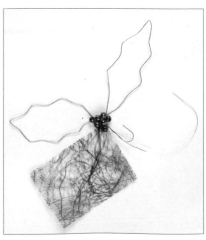

This cracker-shaped card is fun and easy to make.
It is decorated with a poinsettia in delicate, gold angel wire,
complemented by a gold ribbon trim.

Christmas cracker card

wirecraft

- **36in (90cm) 28 gauge (0.3mm) copper wire**
- **6in (15cm) 34 gauge (0.2mm) copper wire**
- **12 seed beads in red and yellow**
- **gold angel wire**

card

- **8 x 6in (20 x 15cm) red card**
- **gold angel wire**
- **two 4in (10cm) lengths wide gold ribbon**
- **two 4in (10cm) lengths narrow gold ribbon**
- **two 12in (30cm) lengths red ribbon**

1 Make the poinsettia following steps 1–8 on page 19.

2 Fold the red card in half lengthways. On the left and right sides of the card, measure 2in (5cm) from the top and the bottom and mark with a pencil. Cut out a triangle on each mark about ⅝in (1.5cm) wide (see left).

3 Draw four zig-zags at the top and bottom of the card with a pencil and cut out the shapes.

4 Glue the lengths of narrow gold ribbon onto the wide gold ribbon. Attach one piece at the top of the card and one at the bottom, wrapping the ends over the edges (see left).

5 Thread the red ribbon through the cut-outs and tie in bows. Trim the ends of the ribbon to neaten.

6 Cut a 1¾ x 1¾in (4.5 x 4.5cm) square of angel wire and glue to the centre of the card. Attach the poinsettia to the square of angel wire with a glue dot (see right).

Make this little bag for those extra gifts such as sweets or smellies. Co-ordinate it with the silver poinsettia card (on page 30) by using silver card for the bag and tag and the same sparkly cord or ribbon.

silver mini bag
and holly leaf tag

wirecraft

- **18in (45cm) 28 gauge (0.3mm) silver wire**
- **6in (15cm) 34 gauge (0.2mm) copper wire**
- **12 red seed beads**
- **silver angel wire**

bag

- **A4 silver card**
- **two 8in (20cm) lengths sparkly cord**

tag

- **spare silver card**
- **silver wire**

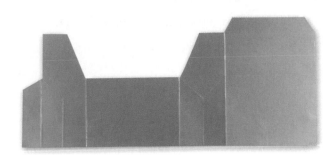

1 Transfer template 1 on page 112 onto the back of the silver card. You will need to increase it by 140%. It is easiest to draw round it and transfer the fold lines using a ruler and pencil.

2 Cut the bag shape out along the cut lines. Punch the holes for the handles – it is easier to do this before the bag has been made up.

3 Score along all the fold lines with your scissors or embossing tool. Crease the mountain and valley folds.

4 Tuck flap (a) into the bag and secure in place using the double-sided tape.

5 Fold flaps (b) down 90° and put a piece of tape on the outside of each tab.

6 Fold flap (c) over and secure to flaps (b). Tuck flap (d) into the inside of the bag. Secure in place with tape.

7 Thread the glittery cord through the holes to make the handles and secure.

8 For the tag, make the holly following the instructions on page 21. Attach it to the piece of card with a glue dot under the berries. Trim the card around the holly to make a pleasing shape.

9 Make a tiny hole at the top of the tag, thread the silver wire through it and twist around the bag handle to secure.

tip

Always lightly score the folding lines first with scissors or an embossing tool. It makes the card much easier to fold.

Use double-sided tape because it will easily stick to the glossy surface and, unlike PVA glue, won't leave smears.

This traditional Christmas decoration is given a twist with a poinsettia in red angel wire and holly leaves in green angel wire to match. Make a tag in co-ordinating colours for a festive place setting.

cracker place setting

wirecraft poinsettia

- **36in (90cm) 28 gauge (0.35mm) red wire**
- **6in (15cm) 34 gauge (0.2mm) copper wire**
- **7 red seed beads**
- **7 yellow seed beads**
- **red angel wire**

wirecraft holly

- **18in (45cm) 28 gauge (0.3mm) green wire**
- **6in (15cm) 34 gauge (0.2mm) copper wire**
- **6 red beads**
- **green angel wire**

tag

- **4 x 5in (10 x 13cm) white card**
- **4 x 5in (10 x 13cm) gold paper**
- **2 x 3½in (5 x 9cm) white card**
- **red ribbon**

1 Make the poinsettia following steps 1–8 on page 19 and the holly following steps 1–5 on page 21.

2 This cracker was made by following the instructions from a cracker kit. These are widely available – you should be able to buy them from your local craft shop or by mail order.

3 To make the tag, glue the gold paper to the white card then fold it in half. Trim the smaller piece of white card with a corner punch and glue to the front of the tag.

4 Tie the ribbon into a bow and attach it to the top of the tag using a piece of double-sided tape.

ideas

Mini crackers make great Christmas tree decorations.

If you make your crackers from a kit, they can be used to wrap small gifts.

red and gold bag, box and tag

This gift bag is made in the same way as the bag on pages 24–25. The tag is lined with red mulberry paper for added detail and is designed to go inside the bag along with the gift. The box makes up a matching set and is easy to make.

wirecraft

- **36in (90cm) 28 gauge (0.3mm) gold wire**
- **6in (15cm) 34 gauge (0.2mm) copper wire**
- **14 red seed beads**
- **gold angel wire**

bag

- **A4 sheet gold card**
- **two 6in (15cm) lengths fancy ribbon**

tag

- **3 x 4in (8 x 10cm) gold card**
- **3 x 4in (8 x 10cm) red mulberry paper**
- **red cord ribbon**

box

- **A4 gold card**
- **fancy ribbon**

1 Make the poinsettia following the instructions on page 19. Increase template 2 on page 112 by 140%. Transfer it onto the back of the gold card. Make the bag up following steps 2–6 on page 25.

2 Thread the ribbon through the holes to make the handles and secure. Attach the poinsettia to the front of the bag with a glue dot.

3 To make the tag, glue the mulberry paper to the wrong side of the gold card. Gently score two lines, 1in (2.5cm) from each edge, using scissors or an embossing tool. Fold these flaps in.

4 Mark two points with a pencil, halfway down the front of each flap, approximately 3/8in (1cm) in from the edge. Punch a hole at each mark. I used a fancy star-shaped punch for that extra festive touch!

5 Thread the cord through the holes to make the handles and tie to finish.

6 To make the box, increase template 3 on page 113 by 116%. Transfer it onto the back of the gold card. Cut along the cut lines using a craft knife or scissors. Score along all the fold lines with the tip of your scissors or an embossing tool.

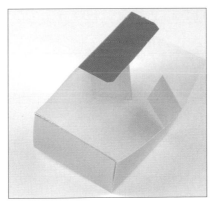

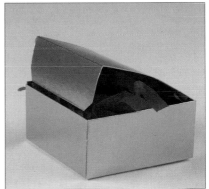

7 Fold all the (a) flaps in and attach to flaps (b) with double-sided tape.

8 Put tape on the insides of flaps (c), tuck them into the box over flaps (b) and secure.

9 Lightly fold in flaps (d) and (e) to form the lid. You could decorate it with ribbon to finish.

It is nice on occasions to buy cards and envelopes that match. This pearlized card comes in an array of pretty colours with matching envelopes. The silver poinsettia perfectly complements the icy colours of the card.

silver poinsettia card

wirecraft

- **36in (90cm) 28 gauge (0.3mm) silver wire**
- **6in (15cm) 34 gauge (0.2mm) silver wire**
- **12 white seed beads (in a combination of plain and pearlescent beads)**
- **silver angel wire**

card

- **8¼ x 4in (21 x 10cm) silver, ready-made card**
- **15in (38cm) festive white or silver ribbon (I used ribbon with a pretty snowflake print)**
- **11in (28cm) sparkly cord**

tips

Angel wire is stronger than mulberry paper and does not tear, but be careful when gluing – darker colours show up glue a lot more than lighter ones.

1 **Make the poinsettia following the instructions on page 19.**

2 **Attach a strip of double-sided tape to the wrong side of the length of white ribbon. Position it on the card in a cross, wrap the ends over the edges and secure in place.**

3 **Position the sparkly cord over the long white ribbon. Overlap the edges of the card and fix the ends in place with pieces of tape.**

4 **Attach the poinsettia at the ribbon join with a glue dot.**

ideas

The poinsettia adds more interest and individuality than a gift bow. Wrap your gift and tie some ribbon around it. If you leave a length of wire 'stem' underneath the poinsettia you can use it to attach the flower to the ribbon.

It is so easy to buy ready made gift bags – there are lots of varieties in the shops. You can customize a plain bag with a wirecraft motif. A gold poinsettia, attached with a glue dot, complements this shop-bought red bag.

Valentine's day

love heart

The heart is a simple, but effective, motif in wirecrafting, and it can be used for so many occasions. You can make them with thin wires and delicate papers, or thick wires and chunky handmade papers.

wirecraft

- **12in (30cm) 21 or 22 gauge (0.8 or 0.7mm) wire**
- **mulberry or handmade paper**
- **3 beads**
- **two lengths of contrasting ribbon**

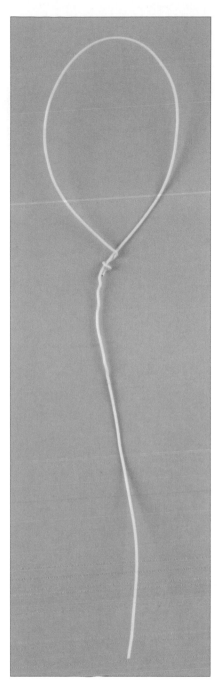

1 Starting at one end of the wire, form it into a large balloon-shape loop, about 2½in (6.5cm) long. Twist the short end of wire around the tail to secure (see left).

2 Push the top of the balloon down into the circle to form the shape of the heart (see right).

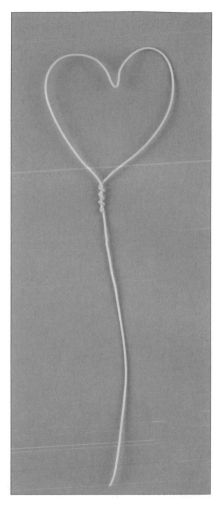

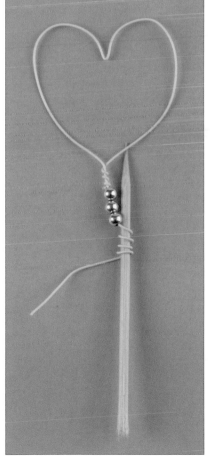

3 Thread the beads onto the wire, then wrap the rest of the wire around a cocktail stick to form a coil (see right). This will hold the beads in place.

4 Cut the paper into a piece slightly larger than the wire heart. Keep a piece of kitchen paper close by. Apply a thin strip of glue to the underside of the wire frame and wipe off any excess with the kitchen paper. Quickly press the paper onto the glued frame.

5 Trim away the excess paper close to the framed edge. Finish by tying the ribbons in a bow above the beads to hide the twisted wire.

The blue and silver paper used on this gift box is pretty and delicate, perfect for wrapping the gift to the one you love.

blue heart box

wirecraft

- 6in (15cm) 21 or 22 gauge (0.8 or 0.7mm) white wire
- silver angel wire
- 3 small silver beads
- silver ribbon

box

- A4 piece of card
- A4 sheet thick paper in blue and silver
- silver tinsel ribbon

1 Make a small wirecraft heart following the instructions on page 35.

2 Attach the blue paper to one side of the card using spray adhesive or a glue stick. Increase template 3 on page 113 by 116% and transfer it onto the wrong side of the card.

3 Cut the box shape out and score along all the fold lines. Fold all the (a) flaps in and attach to flaps (b) with double-sided tape. Put tape on the insides of flaps (c), tuck them into the box over flaps (b) and secure in place.

4 Lightly fold in flaps (d) and (e) to make the lid. Attach the heart to the top with a glue dot and decorate with ribbon.

Once you have mastered the folds, this pretty bag is very straightforward to make.

blue heart bag and tag

wirecraft

- **12in (30cm) 21 or 22 gauge (0.8 or 0.7mm) white wire**
- **silver angel wire**
- **3 silver beads**
- **silver ribbon**

bag

- **A4 size sheet thick paper in blue and silver**
- **spare card**
- **silver tinsel ribbon**

tag

- **2¾ x 3½in (7 x 9cm) card**
- **2¾ x 3½in (7 x 9cm) thick paper in blue and silver**
- **silver tinsel ribbon**
- **silver ribbon or cord**

1 **Make the wirecraft heart, following the instructions on page 35. Increase template 4 on page 114 by 166%. Transfer it onto the back of the paper.**

2 **Lightly score all lines with the embossing tool or tip of scissors. Fold in line (a). Make four holes for the handles on the marked dots, using a hole punch or an eyelet tool and hammer.**

3 **Crease lines (b) and (e) into valley folds and lines (c) and (d) into mountain folds. Fold line (f) to the inside and open the bag out flat again. Overlap and stick the sides together using double-sided tape. One fold (e) should sit inside the other.**

4 **Fold line (f) and lines (h) into the bag. If you have scored the folds, lines (h) should**

automatically fold inwards. If you want to fold the bag flat, crease line (g) at this stage.

5 **Stick the end flaps together with double-sided tape to secure. Cut the spare piece of card just a little smaller than the bottom of the bag. Slide it down into the base of the bag for extra strength.**

6 **Attach the heart to the front of the bag with a glue dot. Finish by threading the tinsel or ribbon through the holes and fold or tie to secure.**

7 **To make the tag, glue the blue paper to the card and fold it in half. Punch a hole in the top left corner and thread through the length of silver cord. Attach a piece of tinsel ribbon to the front of the tag to match the box and bag.**

Valentine's card

*This traditional Valentine's card can be easily personalized.
The wirecraft heart is made using red handmade paper and
little holographic hearts to add some sparkle. These unusual
beads have a textured finish which matches the silver ribbon.*

wirecraft

- 12in (30cm) 21 or 22 gauge
  (0.8 or 0.7mm) red wire
- red handmade paper
- 3 silver beads
- red and silver ribbons
- holographic hearts

card

- 6 x 6in (15 x 15cm) red folded card
- 6 x 6in (15 x 15cm) white
  handmade paper
- holographic hearts

1 Make the wirecraft heart following steps 1–5 on page 35. Glue two or three holographic hearts to the heart motif to finish it off.

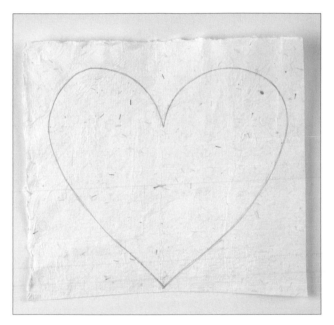

2 Draw a heart shape onto the white handmade paper and carefully cut out. You could draw it freehand if you are confident doing so, or you could lightly fold the paper and draw one half of the heart. Cut out the half with the centre of the heart on the the fold and open it out to make a symmetrical heart.

3 Glue the paper heart to the centre of the red card. Attach the wirecraft heart using a piece of foam tape, which will raise it from the surface of the card.

4 Glue on a few holographic hearts to finish and add your greetings to the right half of the heart.

This is the perfect little box for a Valentine gift, and it makes an ideal accompaniment to the card on page 38. I used a sheet of white handmade paper with glitter flecks embedded and finished with some red ribbon around the edge of the box.

red heart box and tag

wirecraft

- 10in (25cm) 21 or 22 gauge (0.8 or 0.7mm) red wire
- red handmade paper
- 2 silver beads
- red and silver ribbons

box

- 6 x 8in (15 x 20cm) piece of $\frac{1}{16}$in (1.5mm) thick card
- white handmade paper
- 12in (30cm) red ribbon
- spare paper
- acrylic paint (optional)

tag

- 2¼ x 5in (5 x 13cm) red card
- white card
- silver ribbon
- holographic hearts

1 Transfer template 5 on page 115 onto the card. Cut out the corners and score all fold lines with scissors or an embossing tool. You may find it helps to fold thick card when you score the fold lines on both sides.

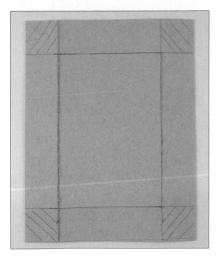

2 Fold up the sides to form the box. Cut the spare paper into four 'tabs', about 1 x 1½in (2.5 x 4cm). Glue a tab around the outside of each corner to secure.

3 Fold up the sides of the lid. Cut four more tabs, about ½ x 1in (1.3 x 2.5cm) and secure around the corners (see left). You will be covering the box and lid so these tabs won't show.

4 If you want to paint the inside of the box and lid, do it at this stage and allow to dry.

5 Cut two pieces of the handmade paper to cover the box and lid. Copy the template and add ⅜in (1cm) all the way round. Rather than cut out the corners this time, cut along one edge of each corner (see page 99).

6 Glue the paper to the base of the box first. Then fold up the ends, tucking the corners round, and glue in place. Glue the remaining sides and trim along the edges using scissors or a craft knife. Repeat with the lid, starting with the top.

7 Glue the ribbon around the lid and attach the heart to the top with foam pads.

8 To make the tag, fold the card in half. Draw a heart (you could do this freehand), cut it out and glue it to the front of the tag. Punch a hole at the top and thread the ribbon through it.

flights of
fantasy party

With such a variety of beads and papers you can make these dragonflies any colour or size you wish. This dragonfly is made using delicate turquoise paper and iridescent beads.

turquoise dragonfly

wirecraft

- **8in (20cm) 28 gauge (0.3mm) copper wire**
- **18in (45cm) 28 gauge (0.3mm) copper wire**
- **7 plated multicoloured beads**
- **2 larger plated multicoloured beads**
- **turquoise green mulberry paper**

ideas

As an alternative to mulberry paper you could use angel hair for the wings, as used on the green dragonfly shown on page 46. You could even use ribbon, as long as it doesn't unravel or fray too much.

1 **Take the 8in (20cm) length of 28 gauge (0.3mm) copper wire. Gently fold the wire in half and thread one bead to sit in the centre of the wire.**

2 Now take one end of the wire and thread a second bead onto it. Hold the bead between your finger and thumb about ¾in (2cm) from the end of the wire. Take the other end of wire and push this through the second bead and gently pull both wires, easing the bead down to sit on the top of the first one.

3 Continue threading the beads in this criss-cross pattern until all seven beads are threaded. Thread the two larger beads in the same way. Cross the two ends of the wire over to form the dragonfly's antennae and trim to the same length.

4 To make the wings, take the 18in (45cm) length of 28 gauge (0.3mm) copper wire and gently fold in half to find the centre point. Wrap the middle of the wire twice around the body between the top two big beads to secure.

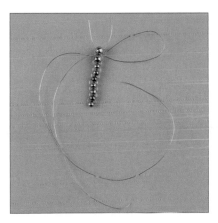

5 Use one half of the wire to make a 1½in (4cm) long loop, starting with the piece of wire closest to the body. Hold the join of the loop really close to the body and twist it three times to secure (see left). Make a second wing on the other side with the longest end of wire.

6 Make two slightly smaller wings either side with the remaining wire. You can then either trim off the ends of the wire at the back, or leave for legs. Rearrange the wings to a pleasing shape.

7 Cut four pieces of mulberry paper, slightly larger than each wing. Apply a thin strip of glue to the underside of the first wing and wipe off any excess. Press the paper onto the glued frame. Trim away the excess paper close to the framed edge. Glue and trim one wing at a time or you will get glue and paper where it shouldn't be!

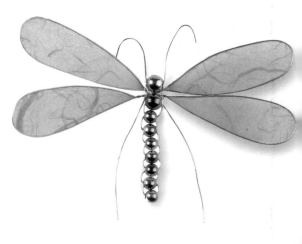

green dragonfly

wirecraft

- **8in (20cm) 28 gauge (0.3mm) copper wire**
- **12in (30cm) 28 gauge (0.3mm) copper wire**
- **20 purple embroidery beads**
- **4 green bugle beads**
- **2 round coloured beads**
- **1 large purple bead**
- **green webbing ribbon**

1 **Take the 8in (20cm) 28 gauge (0.3mm) copper wire and bend it gently in half. Using ten of the purple beads, drop five down each half of the wire.**

2 **Thread a green bugle bead on each end of the wire and then thread both wires through one of the round coloured beads in a criss-cross pattern.**

3 **Thread the rest of the purple beads, five on each side, and then the green bugle beads, one on each side. Thread both wires through the second round coloured bead (see left).**

4 **Thread both wires through the large purple bead following step 2 on page 45. Trim the ends to make the antennae or twist into loops.**

5 **Use the 12in (30cm) length of 28 gauge (0.3mm) copper wire to make the wings, following steps 4–7 on page 45.**

pink and blue dragonfly

wirecraft

- **8in (20cm) 28 gauge (0.3mm) copper wire**
- **12in (30cm) 28 gauge (0.3mm) copper wire**
- **20 pink embroidery beads**
- **20 blue embroidery beads**
- **2 blue square beads**
- **1 large pink square bead**
- **pink mulberry paper**

1 **Take the 8in (20cm) of 28 gauge (0.3mm) copper wire and bend gently in the middle. Thread 20 pink beads onto one half of the wire.**

2 **Thread 20 blue beads onto the second half of wire. Thread both ends of the wire through the two blue beads (see left).**

3 **Thread and knit one pink bead following step 2 on page 45. Trim the ends of the wire to the required length to make the antennae.**

4 **Take the two blue square beads in one hand and twist the body beads until they are coiled to the tail (see right).**

5 **Use the 12in (30cm) of 28 gauge (0.3mm) copper wire to make the wings, following steps 4–7 on page 45.**

These dragonflies can be attached to sticks using coiled wire to make fun place settings and food labels. They look great in mini flowerpots for an outdoor party.

dragonfly place settings

dragonfly stick

- **barbecue stick**
- **10in (25cm) 26 gauge (0.4mm) copper wire**
- **mini flowerpot**
- **dry oasis**
- **miniature peg**
- **fancy fibre or thin cord**

tag

- **various pieces of coloured card**
- **pieces of white card**

1 **Wrap the length of wire around the barbecue stick, pushing the coil together to tighten. When you have wrapped all the wire, bend the end of it to clip around the body of the dragonfly.**

2 Cut the oasis and push down into the flowerpot. Cut some fancy fibre to cover the oasis in the top of the pot.

3 To make the tag, cut a piece of coloured card and a smaller piece of white card and glue them together.

4 Push the dragonfly stick into the middle of the oasis. Write the name on the tag and then peg it to the stick.

ideas

You could use any small container to hold the dragonfly sticks, such as a small jam jar or a lid. Cover it in coloured paper to co-ordinate with the dragonflies. Cut the paper to size, apply PVA glue to the outside of the container with a brush and carefully stick the paper onto the glued surface. Cut the oasis to fit and hide it with some fancy fibre.

This is a such a pretty idea for an outdoor party. Make candle holders using old glass jars – the more shapes and sizes, the better! Use wire or string to make a hanging handle, making sure you wrap it securely around the top of the jar. Then attach your dragonfly to the glass (you could use a glue dot or Blu-Tack). Pop in your tealight and hang from the trees and to decorate your tables. They look stunning in the summer twilight.

This pretty card could be used as an invitation, a birthday card, to say thank you . . . the possibilities are endless! I designed it with a variety of textures and layers to add interest and create a tactile feel.

pink and white
dragonfly card

wirecraft

- 8in (20cm) 28 gauge (0.3mm) copper wire
- 18in (45cm) 28 gauge (0.3mm) copper wire
- 24 pink embroidery beads
- 24 green embroidery beads
- 1 large blue long bead
- 1 large pink round bead
- pink mulberry paper

card

- 6 x 6in (15 x 15cm) white folded card
- 3¼ x 6in (8.5 x 15cm) pink stripy card
- 2½ x 6in (6.5 x 15cm) white stripy card
- 3 x 7in (8 x 18cm) pink angel hair
- 20in (50cm) pink ribbon or cord
- spare pink card

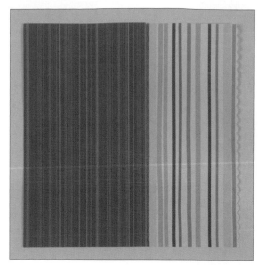

1 The dragonfly is a variation of the pink and blue dragonfly on page 47. Follow steps 1–5 but thread the pink and green beads alternately in threes, and the blue bead in place of the two square blue beads.

2 Trim one edge on each piece of stripy card with decorative scissors. Glue the pink stripy card to the white stripy card, with an overlap of approximately ½in (1.3cm).

3 Place the pink angel hair across the middle of the stripy card. Fold each end over the edge to the underside of the card. Glue the ends in place.

4 Attach the whole piece to the front of the white folded card. Punch three flowers from the spare pink card and glue to the angel hair.

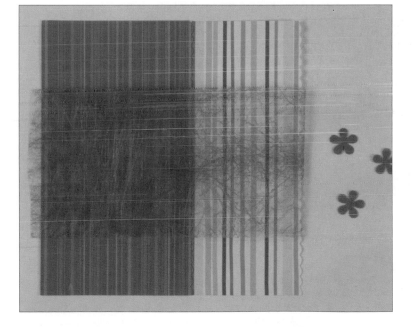

5 Tie the ribbon fibre around the centre of the card and tie in a knot at the front. Attach the dragonfly with a glue dot.

You don't have to just make new bags and boxes: old boxes in plastic and card can be kept and recycled for gift wrapping. This old chocolate box has been transformed with an unusual eight-winged dragonfly.

pink dragonfly box

wirecraft

- 8in (20cm) 28 gauge (0.3mm) copper wire
- 36in (90cm) 28 gauge (0.3mm) copper wire
- 5 pink beads
- 1 green bead

box

- small plastic box
- white mulberry paper
- scrap piece of white paper or card
- yellow accent beads
- rainbow-coloured ribbon

tag

- 2⅜ x 5in (6 x 13cm) white card
- 2⅜ x 5in (6 x 13cm) mulberry paper
- rainbow-coloured ribbon
- piece of white paper or card
- yellow accent beads

1 Make the dragonfly following steps 1–7 on pages 44–45, using the extra long wire to make the eight wings.

2 Cut two pieces of mulberry paper larger than the box and lid. Use a brush to paint the outsides with PVA glue. Place the paper onto the glued surface, easing the paper around the corners (as the paper softens, it will smooth nicely around the curves). When dry, trim the excess paper away from the edges.

3 Use a daisy punch to make two flower shapes out of the white card or paper and glue one on top of the other so that all the petals show through. Colour the petals with pink pastels. Put a small dab of PVA glue in the centre of the flower and sprinkle the yellow accent beads into it.

4 Attach the daisy in one corner and the dragonfly in the other with glue dots. Pop in the goodies and tie the rainbow ribbon around the box.

5 To make the tag, glue the mulberry paper to the card and fold it in half. Thread the ribbon around the centre of the card and tie at the top of the tag. Make a small flower to match the flower on the box and glue it to the front of the tag.

orange dragonfly card

This colourful card is perfect for a birthday.

wirecraft

- **8in (20cm) 28 gauge (0.3mm) copper wire**
- **12in (30cm) 28 gauge (0.3mm) copper wire**
- **9 orange embroidery beads**
- **1 large orange bead**
- **1 large white bead**
- **orange mulberry paper**

card

- **4 x 6in (10 x 15cm) white folded card**
- **4¼ x 5¼in (10.5 x 13.5cm) multicoloured paper**
- **ribbon**

1 **Make the dragonfly following steps 1–7 on pages 44–45.**

2 **Fold the edge of the multicoloured paper over the fold of the card by ½in (1.3cm) and secure in place with double-sided tape.**

3 **Thread the ribbon around the fold of the card and tie at the front in the centre. Attach the dragonfly with a glue dot.**

This fun bag is easy to make and can be filled to the brim with all sorts of things from the party.

orange dragonfly bag

wirecraft

- **8in (20cm) 28 gauge (0.3mm) copper wire**
- **12in (30cm) 28 gauge (0.3mm) copper wire**
- **9 orange embroidery beads**
- **2 large white beads**
- **white/orange mulberry paper**

bag

- **large sheet thick, colourful wrapping paper**
- **yellow/orange ribbon**
- **spare piece of card (optional)**
- **wire**

3 **Lightly score all folding lines using the tip of the scissors or an embossing tool. (Scoring the lines makes them much easier to fold, especially on thick paper and card.) Cut out the bag shape along the cutting lines (see right).**

1 **Make the dragonfly following steps 1–7 on pages 44–45.**

2 **Increase template 6 on page 116 by 160% (or however big you want to make the bag). Transfer it onto the back of the gift wrap.**

4 **Crease down all fold lines. Tuck in flap (a) and secure with tape. Fold in flaps (b) and punch the holes for the handles. Tape the flaps down.**

5 **To make the bottom of the bag, fold in flaps (c) and then flaps (d) on top. Stick in place with tape to secure. If you want to add a little more stability to the base, cut a piece of card slightly smaller than the bottom of the bag and slide it in.**

6 **Thread the ribbon through the handle holes and tie. Make some flowers out of the multicoloured paper using the decorative punch and glue a few to the bag. Attach the dragonfly with a glue dot.**

7 **To make the tag, cut a 2in (5cm) square of the multicoloured paper and punch a tiny hole in the corner. Glue the rest of the flowers to the front of the tag and attach to one of the handles with the piece of wire.**

This quirky gift bag looks like a real handbag at first glance! It is decorated with a motif made in thick silver ribbon and a deep pink feather to finish.

pink handbag

wirecraft

- 12in (30cm) silver wire (any gauge, but not too thick)
- 4in (10cm) silver ribbon
- pink feather

bag

- large sheet textured pink wrapping paper
- small square velcro
- funky fibre

tip

The gift bag folds flat and works well as an envelope with an unusual twist!

1 Make the ribbon bow motif following steps 1–6 on pages 60–61.

2 Increase template 7 on page 117 by 160%. Transfer it onto the back of the wrapping paper. Punch the holes for the handle on the points marked.

3 Score all the fold lines using scissors or an embossing tool. Crease the centre fold, then the end folds. Secure the tabs together with double-sided tape.

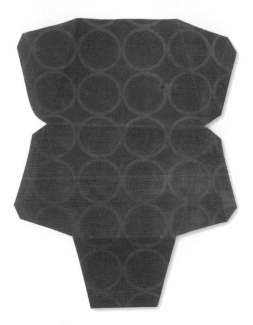

4 Thread the fibres through the holes to make the handle and secure. Attach the square of velcro to the underside of the front flap and to the bag. Attach the motif to the front.

5 Make the tag by cutting out a circle from the pink paper using decorative scissors. Punch a hole, thread the fibre through it and tie it to the bag handle.

wedding day

wirecraft

- **18in (45cm) silver wire (any gauge, but not too thick)**
- **12in (30cm) white netting**
- **4 pearl beads**
- **white feather**

ribbon bow

Ribbon bows are the easiest wirecraft motif to make. You can use any type of ribbon – here I have used pure netting. Use either pearl or aurora beads for these motifs.

tip

The wider the ribbon you use, the larger the beads you will need.

1 **Cut 12in (30cm) of wire and fold it gently in the centre. Thread one bead to the centre fold.**

2 Bring the two ends of the wire together and thread both ends through a second bead (this bead will take a feather later on).

3 Now take one end of the wire and thread a third bead onto it. Hold the bead about ¾in (2cm) from the end of the wire. Take the other end of wire, push this through the third bead and gently pull both wires, easing the bead down to sit on the top of the second one. Thread and knit a fourth bead in the same way. Curl the leftover ends to make the antennae.

4 To make the wings, take the length of netting and find the centre. Place one end of the netting to overlap the centre by ¾in (2cm). Repeat with the other end. Take the leftover wire, which should be 6in (15cm), and wrap it twice around the centre of the netting, catching in the two edges. Twist the ends together to secure. Adjust the wings to the desired shape.

5 To attach the wings to the body, thread the two ends of wire through the second bead from the top (in the same way that you threaded the bead bodies). Take the wires to the back of the wings and secure by twisting together.

6 The feather goes into the second bead from the bottom, so you will need to push the last bead down a little. If the end of the feather is too thick, trim it down a little at an angle. When you are satisfied that the feather will fit, remove it, put a dab of glue on the end and place it in the bead hole at the back.

Pure white ribbon and a fluffy feather give this card a fairylike quality and the heart vellum paper is ideal for a wedding invitation. Once you have practised the ribbon bow motif, this card is incredibly quick and straightforward to make, which means you can make a lot of them!

ribbon bow invitation

wirecraft

- **18in (45cm) silver wire (any gauge, but not too thick)**
- **12in (30cm) white ribbon**
- **4 beads**
- **white feather**

card

- **6in (15cm) square folded card**
- **5½ x 6¼in (14 x 16cm) white heart vellum paper**
- **20in (50cm) thin white ribbon**

tips

Colour co-ordinate the feather and bow to match your colour scheme.

Make smaller matching motifs for the thank you cards after the wedding.

1 Make the ribbon bow following steps 1–6 on pages 60–61.

2 Place the vellum on the card and take it over the fold of the card. Attach it to the back edge of the card with glue or double-sided tape.

3 Tie the length of white ribbon around the card fold and tie, in a knot or a bow, at the front. Attach the ribbon bow with a glue dot.

4 To attach the invite you could cut around the printed text with decorative scissors and glue in place. Or, you could fold the printed invite in half (to make a card within a card) and attach the fold to the inside spine of the card.

This beautiful gift bag is perfect for your bridesmaids' gifts.
Make a miniature version of the bag for a tag to match.

pearl handle bag and tag

wirecraft

- 18in (45cm) silver wire (any gauge, but not too thick)
- 12in (30cm) white netting ribbon
- 5 small pearl beads
- white feather
- pearlescent sequins

bag

- 8¼ x 16in (21 x 40cm) sheet thin, pearlescent or ivory card
- 8¼in (21cm) silver wire
- 32 pearl beads
- velcro tab

wirecraft

- 10in (25cm) silver wire (any gauge, but not too thick)
- 1¼ x 3in (3 x 8cm) white netting
- 4 small pearl beads
- small white feather

tag

- 4 x 6in (10 x 15cm) matching card
- silver wire
- 16 mini pearl beads

2 Increase template 8 on page 118 by 167%. Transfer it onto the back of the card. Cut around the outline and score all the fold lines with scissors or an embossing tool. Crease all mountain and valley folds.

3 Make holes for the handle on the points marked. Crease in flap (a) and fold it flat. Secure with double-sided tape. Secure flap (b) to edge (c) with tape. Fold in flaps (d) and then flaps (e), and tape together. Finally, crease the top flap over to close the bag.

1 Make the wirecraft ribbon bow following steps 1–6 on pages 60–61, using the net ribbon. Glue the sequins to the wings.

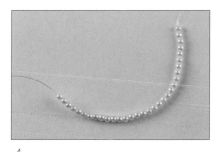

4 Thread the pearl beads onto the length of wire to make the handle. Put the ends of the wire through the holes. Twist the ends together inside the bag to hold in place.

5 Fasten the velcro tab in place to close the flap. Attach the ribbon bow motif to the flap with a glue dot.

tip

If you can't find a piece of pearlescent card bigger than A4, buy a big sheet of pearlescent paper which can then be glued to a sheet of plain card.

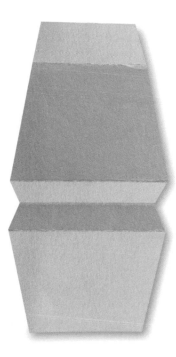

6 For the tag, make a miniature version of the wirecraft ribbon bow on pages 60–61. Transfer template 9 on page 119 onto the back of the pearlescent card. Cut around the outline and gently score all the fold lines.

7 Thread the wire with the pearl beads to make the handle and attach to the tag following step 4. Attach the motif to the front with a glue dot. Secure the flap in place with velcro or a small glue dot.

This unusual wedding place setting uses the same motif and heart vellum paper as the invitation, so it ties in well with the wedding theme. You could also use it as a gift tag.

wedding place setting

wirecraft

- 10in (25cm) silver wire (any gauge, but not too thick)
- 3in (8cm) white ribbon
- 4 small pearl beads
- small white feather

card

- 3½ x 4¼in (9 x 11cm) white card
- 3½ x 4¼in (9 x 11cm) white heart vellum paper

1 Make a miniature version of the wirecraft ribbon bow on pages 60–61, following steps 1–6.

2 Trim the edges of the vellum paper and the white card with decorative scissors. Fold both pieces in half lengthways. Attach the vellum with a small piece of double-sided tape to the back of the fold.

3 Attach the ribbon bow motif in the top left corner with a glue dot. Position it so that the feather extends the card.

To finish your wedding table, these wedding favour bags can be filled with traditional sugared almonds or your preferred little table gift.

wedding favour bag

wirecraft

- 10in (25cm) silver wire (any gauge, but not too thick)
- 3in (8cm) white ribbon
- 4 small pearl beads

bag

- 6in (15cm) square white netting
- 12in (30cm) narrow white ribbon
- silver wire
- favours

1 Make a miniature version of the wirecraft ribbon bow on pages 60–61. This version does not have a feather so follow the instructions from 1 to 5.

2 Place the favours in the centre of the netting and bring the four corners together. Wrap the ribbon around the corners several times to secure and tie in a knot. Attach the ribbon bow motif to the ribbon tie with wire.

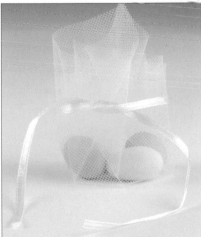

Make this heart using luxurious white handmade paper.
The organza ribbon and pearl beads add a special touch
and the purple leaf makes it really stand out.

heart card

wirecraft

- **12in (30cm) 21 or 22 gauge (0.8 or 0.7mm) white wire**
- **white handmade paper**
- **10in (25cm) white organza ribbon**
- **2 pearl beads**
- **holographic hearts**

card

- **6½ x 6½in (17 x 17cm) white two-fold aperture card**
- **purple skeleton leaf**
- **glitter glue**

tip

Aperture cards (with a frame or 'window') come in many different shapes and sizes. Skeleton leaves are also widely available and come in various colours.

1 **Make the heart following steps 1–5 on page 35. Attach the holographic hearts with dabs of glue.**

2 **Attach the inside of the aperture to the front of the card. Attach the skeleton leaf with glue down the centre rib.**

3 **Attach the heart to the leaf with foam pads to raise it slightly. Dab dots of glitter glue over the background to finish.**

ideas

You could use a skeleton leaf and a wirecraft heart on a wedding album in colours to match the wedding theme.

This box looks so pretty filled with confetti. You could also use it for wedding favours, or simply as a little gift box for that special person. The matching card uses the same heart motif.

pink heart box and card

wirecraft

- 10in (25cm) 21 or 22 gauge white wire
- pink handmade paper
- 2 beads
- ribbons

box

- 6 x 8in (15 x 20cm) piece of ¹⁄₁₆in (1.5mm) thick card
- pink handmade paper
- spare paper for tabs
- acrylic paint (optional)

card

- 3¼ x 10in (8.5 x 25cm) cream card
- pink handmade paper

2 **To make the box, transfer template 10 on page 119 onto the card. Cut out the corners and lightly score all fold lines with the tip of your scissors or an embossing tool.**

3 **Fold up the sides to form the box. Cut the spare paper into four ¾ x 1½in (2 x4cm) tabs. Glue a tab around the outside of each corner.**

4 **Fold up the sides of the lid. Cut four more tabs ½ x ¾in (0.5 x 2cm) and secure around the corners. Paint the inside of the box and lid and allow to dry.**

5 **Cut two pieces of the handmade paper, about ⅜in (1cm) larger than the box and lid. Glue the paper to the base of the box first. Then glue up the sides and trim the excess paper from the edges. Glue the lid in the same way, starting with the top.**

1 **Make the heart motifs following steps 1–5 on page 35.**

6 **To make the card, fold the cream card in half. Cut along the front right-hand edge with decorative scissors. Attach a thin strip of pink paper ⅝ x 3¼in (1.5 x 8.5cm) underneath the decorative edge. It should line up with the underneath edge.**

7 **Cut a 2in (5cm) square out of the pink paper using decorative scissors. Glue this to the front of the card in the middle.**

8 **Finally, attach the wirecraft hearts to the lid of the box and to the front of the card with little foam pads.**

tea party

butterfly

Butterflies are just as easy to make as dragonflies and you can make even more variations in different shapes and sizes. They are perfect for summer birthdays and garden parties, so make a butterfly or two to decorate cards and presents.

wirecraft

- **8in (20cm) 28 gauge (0.3mm) copper wire**
- **12in (30cm) 28 gauge (0.3mm) copper wire**
- **5 pink plated beads**
- **pink mulberry paper**

1 Take the 8in (20cm) length of 28 gauge (0.3mm) copper wire. Gently fold the wire in half and thread one bead to sit in the centre of the wire. Take one end of the wire and thread a second bead onto it. Hold the bead between about ¾in (2cm) from the end of the wire. Taking the other end of the wire, push it through the second bead and gently pull both ends, easing the bead down to sit on top of the first one.

2 Continue threading the rest of the beads in this way. Trim the wire ends to the same length. You could curl the antennae around a cocktail stick, or leave straight. Then take the 12in (30cm) of 28 gauge (0.3mm) copper wire and gently bend in half. Secure the wire to the body of the butterfly by wrapping it twice between the second and third bead (see right).

3 Form a ¾in (2cm) diameter circle on one side of the body and twist twice. Form a second wing on the other side using the longer length of wire. Make two slightly smaller circles with the remaining wire – about ⅝in (1.5cm) – for the second set of wings. Twist the spare wire together at the back of the body to secure and trim off the excess. Form the wings into shape.

4 Trim four pieces of pink mulberry paper, slightly larger than each wing. Apply a thin strip of glue to the underside of the first wing and wipe off any excess. Quickly press the paper onto the glued frame. Trim away the excess paper close to the framed edge. Glue and trim each wing in turn.

leaves

Make leaves to complement your wirecraft flowers and insects. This is the basic leaf shape. You can amend it to make ivy (see page 83), or just experiment and see what you come up with!

- 12in (30cm) 28 gauge (0.3mm) green wire
- green mulberry paper
- green pen

tip

Use pastel chalks on any mulberry paper to create a more realistic look.

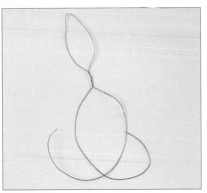

1 Find the centre of the wire and use it to form a loop 1⅜in (3.5cm) long. Twist the wire in to a ⅜in (1cm) stem. Form a second and third loop on the remaining ends of wire and twist a stem for each one. Twist the leftover wire into one stem.

2 Pinch the point of each loop, then open out again in the centre to form the leaf shape. Cut three pieces of green mulberry paper larger than each leaf and attach in the usual way. Draw in the veins with a green pen to finish.

lavender bags

These pretty paper sachets make lovely lavender bags, and the wirecraft motifs add an unusual finishing touch. During the summer months I collect the lavender flowers, tie the stems together and place them upside down in a paper bag to dry for a month or two.

bag

- **4 x 7in (10 x 18cm) piece handmade paper**
- **dried lavender**
- **wirecraft motif**

tips

Remember to remove the flower heads from the stems before use.

Lavender bags make lovely presents or party favours. You could even use them for gift tags or place settings.

1 Make the motifs for the lavender bags. These bags have been decorated with a pink butterfly (page 74), a purple flower (pages 14–15) and a blue dragonfly (pages 44–45).

2 Cut the paper to size using decorative scissors. Cut off the top corners to a depth of 1³⁄₈in (3.5cm). Crease in 2¹⁄₂in (6.5cm), then crease the top over to form the envelope shape.

3 Unfold and place a thin strip of double-sided tape along the edges of the middle section. Fold the bottom section in and secure in place.

4 Add a few heads of dried lavender and glue the flap shut. Add your wirecraft motif with a glue dot.

5 When you have made your lavender bags, store them in clear cellophane gift bags, which will help keep the lavender fresh until the bags are needed.

This simple card uses a lovely green skeleton leaf and pink flowers, which makes the ideal setting for a butterfly!

pink butterfly card

wirecraft

- 6in (15cm) 28 gauge (0.3mm) copper wire
- 12in (30cm) 28 gauge (0.3mm) copper wire
- 5 pink plated beads
- pink mulberry paper
- pearl dimensional paint

card

- 6in (15cm) square, folded white card
- 6in (15cm) square, pink mulberry paper
- 4½ in (11.5cm) square, white card
- large green skeleton leaf
- 3 pink beads (to match the body of the butterfly)
- spare pink mulberry paper
- spare white paper or card

1 Make the butterfly following steps 1–4 on pages 74–75. Decorate its wings with a few dots of pearl dimensional paint.

2 Wet tear the pink mulberry paper so that it is just smaller than the white card. For this you need a clean paintbrush. Wet the brush and use it to draw the outline on the paper, then gently tear the pieces apart (see right). Fluff the edges when dry.

3 Glue the pink mulberry paper to the card, and then attach the square of white card on top. Use a glue stick to attach the skeleton leaf to the square of white card (see left).

4 Glue the spare pink mulberry paper to some white paper or card. This will strengthen it to make the flowers. Punch three flower shapes using a flower punch and glue them to the front of the card. Glue the beads to the centre of the flowers and attach the butterfly with a glue dot.

round flower box

The delicate five-petal flower on this box is made with silver wire and pink mulberry paper and is placed over three green leaves.

wirecraft flower

- **14in (35cm) 28 gauge (0.3mm) silver wire**
- **6in (15cm) 34 gauge (0.2mm) silver wire**
- **12 green seed beads**
- **pink mulberry paper**

wirecraft leaves

- **12in (30cm) 28 gauge (0.3mm) green wire**
- **green mulberry paper**

box

- **A4 sheet of thick card**
- **A4 sheet petal paper**
- **acrylic paint**

1 Make the flower following steps 1–10 on pages 14–15. Make the leaves following steps 1–2 on page 75.

2 **Increase template 11 on page 120 by 130%. Transfer it onto to the card. Cut the pieces out.**

3 **To make the lid, form piece (a) into a circle around piece (b) and join the ends together with tape. Brush PVA glue around the join both inside and outside the box to hold the two pieces together and allow this to dry.**

4 **Make the box in the same way, forming piece (c) around piece (d). Glue around the join and allow to dry.**

5 **Paint inside the lid and inside the box with acrylic paint and allow to dry. The paint will help to strengthen the joints.**

6 **For the cover, cut the petal paper into four pieces for parts (a) to (d). The round pieces need a ⅜in (1cm) 'allowance' all the way round. The long pieces need an extra ⅜in (1cm) added to the ends.**

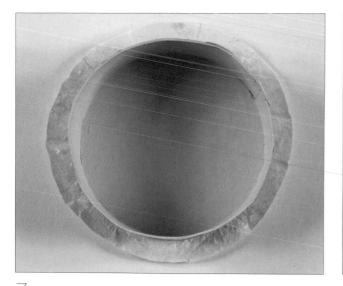

7 **Apply glue to the top of the lid and place on the wrong side of its corresponding paper piece. Turn up the edges of the paper around the lid sides, smoothing it flat as you go. You can do this by either folding the paper or cutting notches into it. Glue in place.**

8 **Cover the box base in the same way. Glue the outer side of the lid, and place its corresponding paper strip round it. The join should overlap by ⅜in (1cm). Trim the edges if needed and then cover the box sides. Glue the wirecraft leaves and flowers to the box lid to finish.**

The flower made on page 14 can be used to decorate this pretty card, which couldn't be simpler to make. Skeleton leaves are gorgeous – you can buy them in many interesting shapes and colours and they need no other embellishment.

lilac flower card

wirecraft

- 18in (45cm) 28 gauge (0.3mm) copper wire
- 6in (15cm) 34 gauge (0.2mm) copper wire
- 12 yellow seed beads
- lilac mulberry paper

card

- 5in (13cm) square white folded card
- 2 green skeleton leaves

1 **Make the flower following steps 1–10 on pages 14–15.**

2 **Attach the skeleton leaves to the card with dabs of glue. Attach the flower to the centre with a mini glue dot.**

ideas

Ivy is another useful wirecraft technique – great to tuck under your flowers or to use on its own. I have used it here on an old box, re-covered in lemon paper, with a yellow ribbon to open it. It's a great way of recycling old boxes for gift packaging.

Make the flower using yellow mulberry paper and white beads, and keep the petals round instead of pinching the tips.

1 To make the ivy, start by making the basic leaf shape (follow steps 1–2 on page 75). Pinch the points of each loop to start the shaping. Shape the sides into points as shown. Use a green pastel chalk and a pen to colour the leaves and draw in the veins to create a realistic look.

2 Make a tag in the same paper you used to cover the box. Cut the paper and a piece of card to 2 x 6in (5 x 15cm). Glue the paper to the card and fold it in half. Punch a hole in the top left-hand corner and tie a length of ribbon through it to finish.

This beautiful handmade paper adds a textual element to cards and giftwrap. The card is decorated with a pink dragonfly, perched upon some dried bougainvillaea petals.

dragonfly card, box and tag

wirecraft

- 8in (20cm) 28 gauge (0.3mm) copper wire
- 18in (45cm) 28 gauge (0.3mm) copper wire
- 6 pink beads
- 2 larger plated multicoloured beads
- pink mulberry paper

card

- 6¼ x 8½in (16 x 22cm) handmade petal paper
- 5¾ x 8¼in (14.5 x 21cm) white card (for insert)
- 18in (45cm) pink raffia
- dried bougainvillaea petals

tip

I collected the bougainvillaea petals on holiday in Kenya one year, but you can buy them already dried and pressed.

1 Make the dragonfly following steps 1–7 on pages 44–45.

2 Trim the edges of the petal paper with deckle-edged scissors. Fold this and the white card in half, and insert the card inside the petal paper.

tip

During the summer months, collect petals and thin flowers from your garden. Gently pick the petals or leaves before any damage from rain or insects. Space them out between two pieces of blotting paper in the pages of a thick book and leave this somewhere warm and dry, with a heavy object on top, for about two weeks. You could also buy a traditional flower press.

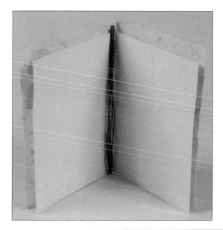

3 Wrap the length of pink raffia around the fold and tie in a knot at the front. Trim the ends to neaten. This should hold the card and paper together but you could add a little glue as well.

4 Glue the bougainvillaea petals to the front of the card using white PVA glue and a paintbrush. Then add a mix of watered-down glue to cover, seal and protect them. Allow this to dry and attach the dragonfly on top with a glue dot.

ideas

This gift tag has been made with bougainvillaea petals to match the dragonfly card. The box is covered with a paper which has bougainvillaea petals embedded in it. Use the same pink raffia ribbon to tie around the box.

Cut the paper into a 3 x 4in (8 x 10cm) tag with decorative scissors. Attach three bougainvillaea petals and allow to dry. Punch a hole in the corner and tie a length of pink raffia through it.

wedding anniversary

feather
butterflies

Feather butterflies are great fun to make. You can match or contrast the feathers and add glitter glue or sequins to the wings.

wirecraft

- **12in (30cm) silver wire**
- **18in (45cm) silver wire**
- **mulberry paper**
- **14 beads**
- **1 feather**

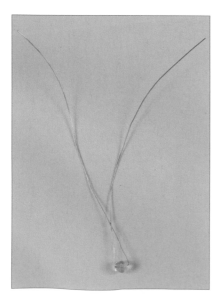

1 **Take the 12in (30cm) length of wire and fold it gently in the centre. Thread one bead to the centre fold (see left). Bring the two ends of the wire together and thread both ends through a second bead.**

2 **Take one end of the wire and thread a third bead onto it. Hold the bead between your finger and thumb, about ¾in (2cm) from the end of the wire. Take the other end of wire, push this through the third bead and gently pull both wires, easing the bead down to sit on the top of the second one. Thread the fourth bead in the same way.**

3 Trim the antennae or curl. Take the 18in (45cm) length of wire, find the middle and wrap it twice between the two top beads until secure.

4 Form one large wing on either side by holding the end of the wire at the back of the body, twist the wires together to form one large loop. Make a second loop on other side.

5 Shape the wings and experiment a little! You can make them any shape you like – short, long, thin or rounded. For the wings here I pinched the top and bottom and eased out the middle to make a long, elegant fairylike wing.

6 Cut two pieces of mulberry paper, slightly larger than each wing. Apply a thin strip of glue to the underside of the first wing and wipe off any excess. Quickly press the paper onto the glued frame. Trim away the excess paper close to the framed edge. Glue and trim the second wing. Decorate the wings with glitter glue or sequins.

7 Attach a feather or two to the second bottom bead. If the end of the feather is too thick, trim it down a little at an angle. When you are satisfied with the fit, remove it, put a dab of glue on the end and place back into the bead hole.

ideas

Add arms and legs made with beaded wire, and turn your feather butterfly into a fairy – perfect for the top of the Christmas tree!

This big gift bag is ideal for those larger presents.
It is adorned with two colourful feather butterflies and
a heart-shaped tag to finish it off.

purple butterfly bag

wirecraft

- 2 A3 size sheets of handmade paper
- 4 flower eyelets (optional)
- fancy cord or ribbon
- spare card

tag

- matching piece of handmade paper
- matching cord or ribbon

1 Make the feather butterfly following steps 1–7 on pages 88–89.

2 This gift bag follows the same principle as the blue heart bag on page 37, but has two side joins instead of one. Increase template 12 (pieces 1 and 2) on page 121 by 300%. Join the pieces together on the marked line and secure with tape, to make up a full-size template. Transfer this twice, one on the back of each piece of A3 paper.

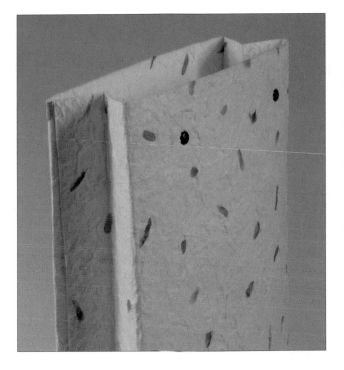

3 Cut out the two pieces along the cut lines. Lightly score all lines with the embossing tool or tip of scissors. Fold lines (a) into valley folds and lines (b) into mountain folds. Overlap each side so that one line (a) sits inside the other line (a). Secure the joins in place with double-sided tape.

4 Fold in line (c). Make four holes for the handles on the marked dots, using a hole punch or an eyelet tool and hammer. If using eyelets, fasten them to the holes.

5 Crease lines (d) and (e) into the bag. Lines (e) should automatically fold inwards. Stick the end flaps together with double-sided tape to secure. Cut the spare piece of card just a little smaller than the bottom of the bag. Slide it down to the bottom of the bag for extra strength.

6 Thread the cord through the holes to make the handles and secure. To make the tag, draw a heart shape onto a piece of matching paper and cut out. Punch a hole in the top and attach it to one of the handles. Finally, attach the feather butterflies to the front of the bag with glue dots.

A box made in silver is perfect for a silver wedding anniversary. You could also make it in red for a ruby wedding or gold for a golden anniversary present.

silver box and tag

wirecraft

- 6in (15cm) 28 gauge (0.3mm) silver wire
- 3½in (9cm) silver netting ribbon
- 4 silver beads
- 1 silver feather
- 1 white feather

box

- 2 A4 sheets card
- silver metallic paper
- silver paint (optional)
- spare paper

wirecraft

- 3in (8cm) 28 gauge (0.3mm) silver wire
- 1¼in (3cm) silver netting ribbon
- 4 small silver beads
- 1 small white feather

tag

- 2½ x 4in (6.5 x 10cm) white card
- 2½ x 4in (6.5 x 10cm) matching silver paper
- silver cord

3 **Fold up the sides to form the box. Cut the spare paper into four tabs, about 1 x 1½in (2.5 x 4cm). Glue a tab around the outside of each corner to secure.**

4 **Fold up the sides of the lid. Cut four more tabs, about ½ x 1in (1.3 x 2.5cm) and secure around the corners. You will be covering the box and lid so these tabs won't show.**

5 **Paint the inside of the box and lid with silver acrylic paint. Allow to dry.**

6 **Cut two pieces of the silver paper to cover the box and lid. Copy the template and add ⅜in (1cm) all the way round. Cut along one edge of each corner (see page 99).**

1 **Make the ribbon bow motif following steps 1–6 on pages 60–61. Twist the excess wires at the back of the motif but do not trim off.**

2 **Increase template 13 on page 122 by 217%. Transfer it onto the card. Cut out the corners and score all fold lines with scissors or an embossing tool. It often helps to score thick card on both sides.**

7 **Glue the paper to the base of the box first. Then fold up the ends, tucking the corners round, and glue in place. Glue the remaining sides and trim along the edges using a craft knife or scissors. Repeat with the lid, starting with the top.**

8 **After you have wrapped the gift and put it in the box, tie the ribbon around it and tuck the motif into the knot using the bit of twisted wire.**

9 **For the tag, make a miniature version of the motif following steps 1–6 on pages 60–61. Glue the silver paper to the white card and fold it in half. Punch a hole in the corner and thread the cord through. Attach the motif with a glue dot.**

- 6in (15cm) 28 gauge
  (0.3mm) silver wire
- 3½in (9cm) silver
  netting ribbon
- 4 large silver beads
- 4 purple feathers

card

- 6in (15cm) square
  green folded card
- 5 x 6in (13 x 15cm)
  patterned paper
- purple fibres

purple feather card

This striking card is decorated with a feather butterfly
made using four feathers in different purple shades.
It is an ideal card for a wedding anniversary.

1 Make the motif following steps 1–6 on pages 60–61. You will need to use large beads with a big enough hole for all the feathers.

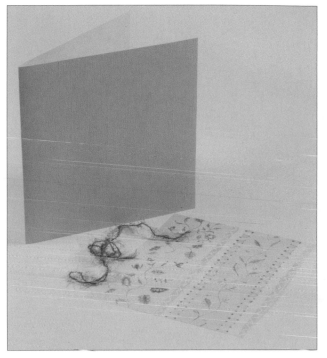

2 Trim the patterned paper with decorative scissors and glue to the front of the card.

3 Wrap the fibres around the fold of card and tie at the front. Attach the motif to the middle of the card.

ideas

You could also use these fantasy creatures as decorations – hang them from a window by attaching nylon thread to one of the beads.

This pretty pink bag is suitable for a whole range of occasions, not just wedding anniversaries. Once you have established the method of making the bags you can develop the templates into all shapes and sizes.

pink leaf bag and tag

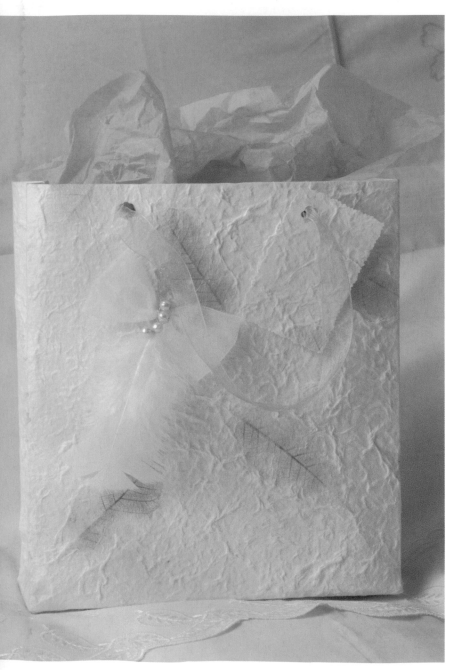

wirecraft

- 18in (45cm) silver wire (any gauge but not too thick)
- 7in (18cm) white organza ribbon
- 4 pink beads
- 1 pink feather

bag

- 2 pieces of pink handmade paper
- pink ribbon
- eyelets (optional)

1 Make the ribbon bow following steps 1–6 on pages 60–61.

2 This gift bag is also made with two side joins instead of one. Increase template 14 on page 123 by 200%. Transfer it onto the back of each piece of paper.

3 Cut out the two pieces along the cut lines. Lightly score all lines with the embossing tool or tip of scissors. Fold lines (a) into valley folds and lines (b) into mountain folds. Overlap each side so that one line (a) sits inside the other line (a). Secure the joins in place with double-sided tape.

4 Fold in line (c). Make four holes for the handles on the marked dots, using a hole punch or eyelet tool and hammer. If using eyelets, fasten them to the holes at this stage.

5 Crease lines (d) and (e) into the bag. Lines (e) should automatically fold inwards. Stick the end flaps together with double-sided tape to secure. Cut the spare piece of card just a little smaller than the bottom of the bag. Slide it down to the bottom of the bag for extra strength. Fold in line (f) if you want the bag flat.

6 To make the tag, cut a 2 x 3in (5 x 8cm) piece of matching paper and punch a hole in the top left corner. Thread the ribbon through the holes for the handles, threading one end through the hole in the tag as well. Tie the ends to secure, and attach the ribbon bow motif with a glue dot.

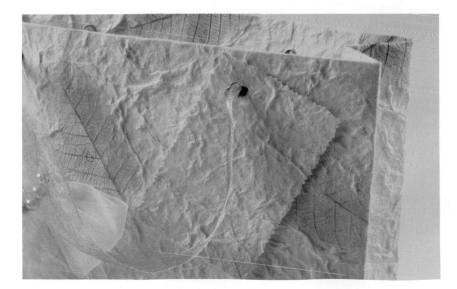

This is another useful box, covered in pretty handmade paper. Make a ribbon bow with a bright pink feather to make it really stand out.

pink feather box and tag

wirecraft

- 18in (45cm) silver wire (any gauge but not too thick)
- 3½in (9cm) silver netting ribbon
- 4 pearlescent beads
- 1 pink feather

box

- A4 sheet card
- pink handmade paper
- pink acrylic paint (optional)
- spare paper

1 Make the ribbon bow motif following instructions 1–6 on pages 60–61.

2 Increase template 15 on page 124 by 150%. Transfer it onto the card. Cut out the corners and score all fold lines with the tip of your scissors or an embossing tool.

3 Fold up the sides to form the box. Cut the spare paper into four tabs, about 1 x 1½in (2.5 x 4cm). Glue a tab around the outside of each corner to secure.

4 Fold up the sides of the lid. Cut four more tabs, about ½ x 1in (1.3 x 2.5cm) and secure around the corners. Paint the inside of the box and lid with pink acrylic paint. Allow to dry.

5 Cut two pieces of the paper to cover the box and lid. Copy the template and add ⅜in (1cm) all the way round. Cut along one edge of each corner as shown.

6 Glue the paper to the base of the box first. Fold up the ends, tucking the corners round, and glue in place. Glue the remaining sides and trim along the edges using a craft knife or scissors. Repeat with the lid, starting with the top.

7 Attach the motif to the lid with a glue dot. To make the tag, cut a piece of matching paper 2½ x 3in (6.5 x 8mm) using decorative scissors. Fold in half, make a hole in the top corner and thread a piece of cord through it.

baby

The pram is a little more complicated than the other techniques so far. It can be made from most wires but the thicker gauges are better.

pram

wirecraft

- **11in (28cm) 21 gauge (0.8mm) white wire**
- **6in (15cm) black wire (any gauge)**
- **mulberry paper**
- **thick pen or glue lid**

  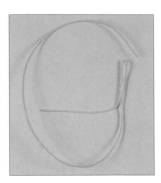

1 **Take the 11in (28cm) length of wire and measure 1½in (4cm) from the left end of the wire. With finger and thumb form a 90° bend.**

2 **To form the handle, measure 1in (2.5cm) from the bend and fold the wire, doubling it back on itself.**

3 **For the body of the pram, form the remaining length of wire down into a half circle, about 1in (2.5cm), and back up to overlap the left-hand side of the wire.**

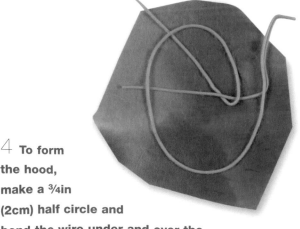

4 **To form the hood, make a ¾in (2cm) half circle and bend the wire under and over the 'start line'. Leave the extended piece of wire until the paper is glued to the frame.**

5 **Cut the paper into a piece slightly larger than the pram shape. Apply a thin strip of glue to the underside of the wire frame and wipe off any excess with kitchen paper. Quickly press the paper onto the glued frame. Trim the paper and the overlapping wires at the same time, with an old pair of scissors.**

6 **Bend the tip of the handle over gently, or for a different look, twist the wire with pliers and then bend the tip. Take care not to unstick the paper when shaping the handle.**

7 Use the 6in (15cm) black wire to form the wheels. Wrap the wire round the pen or glue lid to form a circle and twist the ends to secure.

8 As close to the first circle as possible, wrap the wire round the lid to make a second wheel and twist to secure. Trim the ends off. The wheels can be attached when gluing the pram to your project with a glue dot, either under or over the pram.

The pin is an easy wirecraft technique, and great fun to make!

pin

wirecraft

- **12in (30cm) 21 gauge (0.8mm) white wire**
- **14 coloured beads**
- **paper**
- **3 pens or pencils in different sizes.**

1 Take the 12in (30cm) length of wire and find the centre. Wrap the centre around the biggest pen casing to form a complete circle. The leftover ends of wire form the sides of the pin.

2 Thread seven beads onto each side of the pin. You can vary the number of beads according to the size of the pin you make.

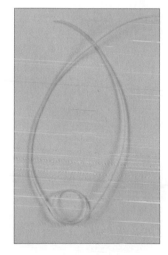

3 You will need the two smaller pens for this stage. Wrap the end of the right wire round the larger of the two pens to form a circle. Shape the end of the left wire into a circle around the smaller pen.

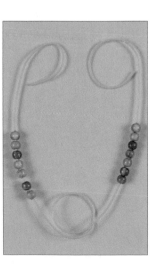

4 Indent the bottom of the larger circle to shape. Flatten the smaller circle a little and then place it over the top of the bigger circle.

5 Cut the paper into a piece slightly larger than the top of the pin. Apply a thin strip of glue to the underside of the wire frame and wipe off any excess with kitchen paper. Quickly press the paper onto the glued frame. Trim away the excess paper close to the edge.

This little box is a great way to send a piece of christening cake to an absent guest, or to use for a gift to a new baby.

pink gingham box

wirecraft

- 11in (28cm) 21 gauge (0.8mm) white wire
- 6in (15cm) black wire (any high gauge)
- pink mulberry paper

box

- A4 sheet thin card
- pink gingham mulberry paper
- 2in (5cm) square pink handmade paper
- gingham ribbon

tag

- pink gingham mulberry paper
- spare white paper or card
- gingham ribbon

tip

If using a fine, light-coloured mulberry paper, it may be better to glue it to some white paper first. Mulberry paper on its own has a tendency to split or tear and it can also show the colour of the box underneath.

1 Make the wirecraft pram following steps 1–8 on pages 102–103.

2 To make the box, increase template 3 on page 113 by 116%. Transfer it onto the back of the card. Cut along the cut lines using a craft knife or scissors. Score along all the fold lines with the tip of your scissors or an embossing tool.

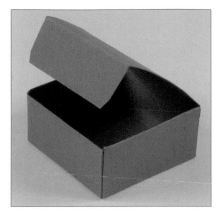

3 Fold all the (a) flaps in and attach to flaps (b) with double-sided tape. Put tape on the insides of flaps (c), tuck them into the box over flaps (b) and secure. Lightly fold in flaps (d) and (e) to form the lid.

4 To make the box cover, increase template 16 on page 125 by 184% and transfer it onto the back of the gingham paper. Cut it out and make cuts along the cut lines. Glue sides (a) and (b), folding the corners around the front and back as shown. Glue flap (c) to the front. Fold the lid piece over and glue in place starting at the back.

5 Trim the excess paper from all the edges. Trim the edges of the handmade paper square with decorative scissors and glue to the top of the box. Attach the wheels to this with foam pads and attach the pram on top. Tie the ribbon into a bow and secure with a glue dot.

6 To make the tag, glue a piece of the gingham mulberry paper to the spare piece of card and trim it into a 2in (5cm) square using decorative scissors. Punch a hole in the corner and tie the ribbon through it.

This larger gift bag is suitable for baby clothes or a soft toy.
Choose plain paper so that you can make a matching card.

pin bag and tag

wirecraft

- 12in (30cm) 21 gauge (0.8mm) white wire
- 14 coloured beads
- multicoloured mulberry paper

bag

- 2 sheets giftwrap
- multicoloured mulberry paper
- 2 x 4in (5 x 10cm) matching giftwrap
- wide ribbon

tag

- multicoloured mulberry paper
- 2in (5cm) square matching giftwrap
- 2in (5cm) square white card
- thin ribbon

1 Make the pin following steps 1–5 on page 103.

2 Increase template 17 on page 125 by 220% and transfer it onto the back of each piece of giftwrap.

3 Cut out the two pieces and lightly score all lines. Fold lines (a) into valley folds and lines (b) into mountain folds. Overlap each side so that one line (a) sits inside the other line (a). Secure the joins in place with double-sided tape.

4 Fold in line (c). Make four holes for the handles on the marked dots, using a hole punch or eyelet tool and hammer. If using eyelets, fasten them to the holes. Crease lines (d) and (e) into the bag. Lines (e) should automatically fold inwards. Stick the end flaps together with double-sided tape to secure.

5 Cut the spare piece of card just a little smaller than the bottom of the bag. Slide it down to the bottom of the bag for extra strength. Fold in line (f) if you want the bag flat. Tie the ribbon through the holes for the handles.

6 Wet-tear the mulberry paper to make a 2½ x 4½in (6.5 x 11.5cm) piece using a damp paint brush. Fluff the edges up once dry and glue it to the front of the bag. Trim the edges of the giftwrap with decorative scissors and glue it to the mulberry paper. Attach the pin with a glue dot.

7 Make a smaller version of the pin for the gift tag, using a pencil for shaping. Wet-tear the mulberry paper into a 2½in (6.5cm) square. Glue the square of giftwrap to the top of the mulberry paper and the white card to the back (for writing your greetings). Punch a hole in the corner and thread a ribbon to attach.

The card matches the bag on page 106. It's fun to have a matching set and it makes the gift even more special.

pin card

wirecraft

- 12in (30cm) 21 gauge (0.8mm) white wire
- 14 coloured beads
- multicoloured mulberry paper

card

- 6 x 8¼in (15 x 21cm) white card
- 6 x 8¼in (15 x 21cm) giftwrap
- 2¾ x 4½in (7 x 11.5cm) matching giftwrap
- multicoloured mulberry paper
- 16in (40cm) thin ribbon

1 **Make the pin following steps 1–5 on page 103.**

2 **Trim the edges of the piece of giftwrap with decorative scissors and attach it to the folded white card, near the fold at the back, with a piece of double-sided tape.**

3 **Wet-tear the mulberry paper into a 2¾ x 4½in (7 x 11cm) piece and glue it to the card. Trim the edges of the giftwrap with decorative scissors and glue it to the mulberry paper. Attach the pin with a glue dot and tie the ribbon around the fold to finish.**

I made this pram in traditional pale blue – the same blue as on the card – and added a cute fluffy trim.

pram card

wirecraft

- **11in (28cm) 21 gauge (0.8mm) white wire**
- **6in (15cm) black wire (any high gauge)**
- **blue mulberry paper**

card

- **5 x 10in (13 x 25cm) white card**
- **3½in (9 cm) square blue handmade paper**
- **3in (8cm) square cream paper**
- **fancy fibre**

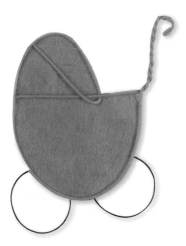

1 Make the pram following steps 1–8 on pages 102–103. On this pram I made a twisted handle.

2 Fold the white card in half. Trim the edges of the blue paper with decorative scissors. Glue the blue square to the front of the card to form a diamond shape.

3 Glue the cream paper to the centre of the blue paper. Attach the wheels to the centre of the cream paper with foam pads and stick the pram on top, using extra foam pads if necessary.

4 Finally, wrap the fancy fibre ribbon around the centre fold and tie at the front.

There are some fabulous handmade papers available these days. This is a very modern gift bag and tag for a new baby, and it makes a refreshing change from the traditional pastels.

pram bag and tag

wirecraft

- **11in (28cm) 21 gauge (0.8mm) white wire**
- **6in (15cm) black wire (any gauge)**
- **multicoloured handmade paper**

bag

- **A4 sheet multicoloured handmade paper**
- **yellow eyelets (optional)**
- **silver cord**
- **spare card**

tag

- **3½ x 4¾in (9 x 12cm) multicoloured handmade paper**
- **2½ x 4¼in (6.5 x 11cm) white card**
- **yellow eyelets (optional)**
- **silver cord**

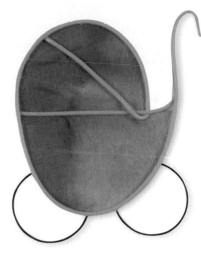

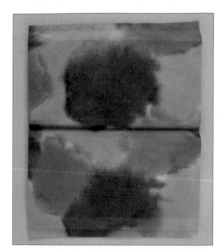

1 Make the wirecraft pram following instructions 1–8 on pages 102–103.

2 Increase template 4 on page 114 by 166%. Transfer it onto the back of the paper. Lightly score all lines with the embossing tool or the tip of a pair of scissors.

3 Fold in line (a). Make four holes for the handles on the marked dots, using a hole punch or eyelet tool and hammer. Secure the eyelets in place, if using them.

4 Crease lines (b) and (e) into valley folds and lines (c) and (d) into mountain folds. Fold line (f) to the inside and open the bag out flat again. Overlap and stick the sides together using double-sided tape. One fold (e) should sit inside the other.

5 Fold line (f) and lines (i) into the bag. If you have scored the folds, lines (i) should automatically fold inwards. If you want to fold the bag flat, crease line (g) at this stage.

6 Stick the end flaps together with double-sided tape to secure. Cut the spare piece of card just a little smaller than the bottom of the bag. Slide it down to the bottom of the bag for extra strength. Tie the cord through the holes to make the handles.

7 To make the tag, trim the edges of the multicoloured paper and card with decorative scissors. Fold both pieces in half and glue the white card to the inside of the tag.

8 Punch a hole in the top left corner of the tag (on the first half only) and attach the eyelet, if using. Attach the wheels and pram to the front of the tag with foam pads. Thread the cord through the hole and attach it to one of the bag handles to finish.

templates

1 silver mini gift bag **photocopy this template at 140%**

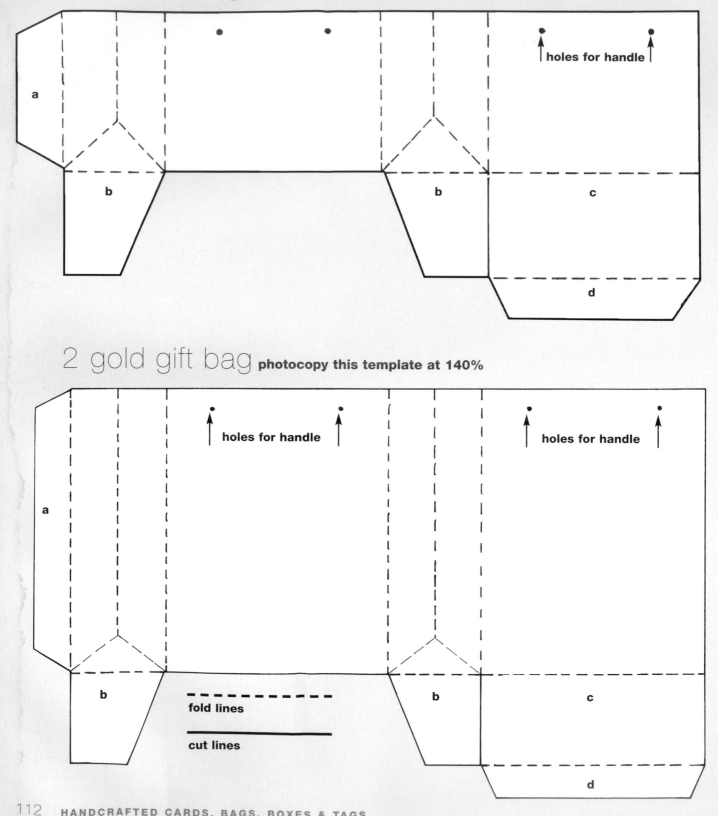

2 gold gift bag **photocopy this template at 140%**

3 blue heart box photocopy this template at 116%

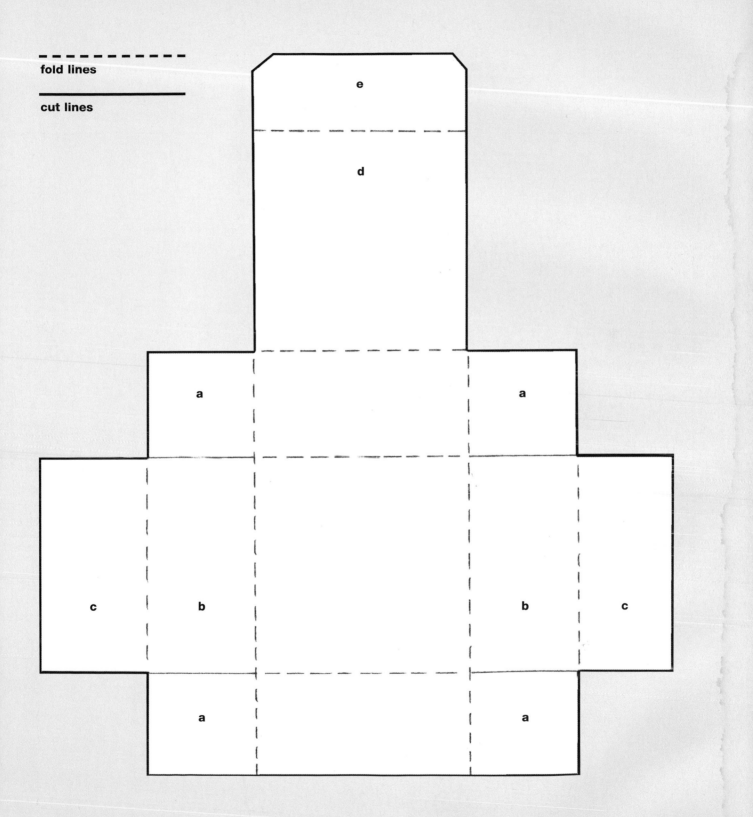

4 blue heart and pram bag photocopy this template at 166%

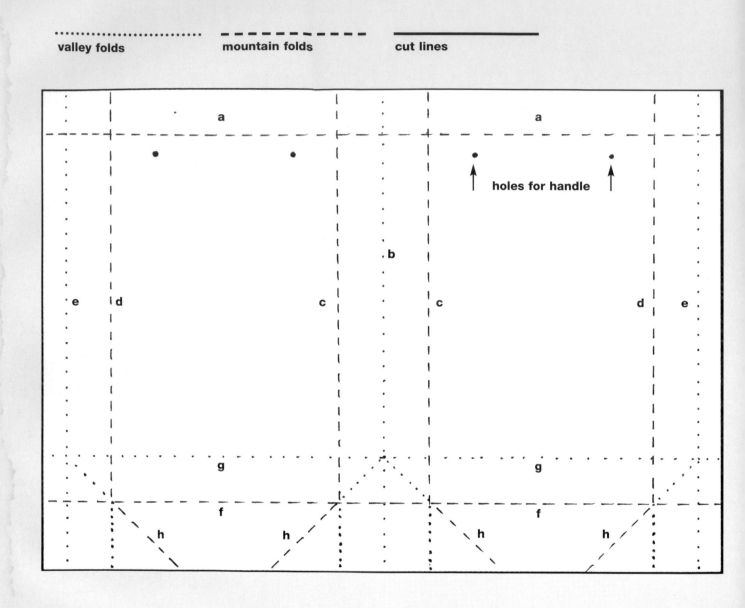

valley folds ······ mountain folds – – – cut lines ——

holes for handle

5 red heart box (actual size)

fold lines - - - - - - - - **cut lines** ———

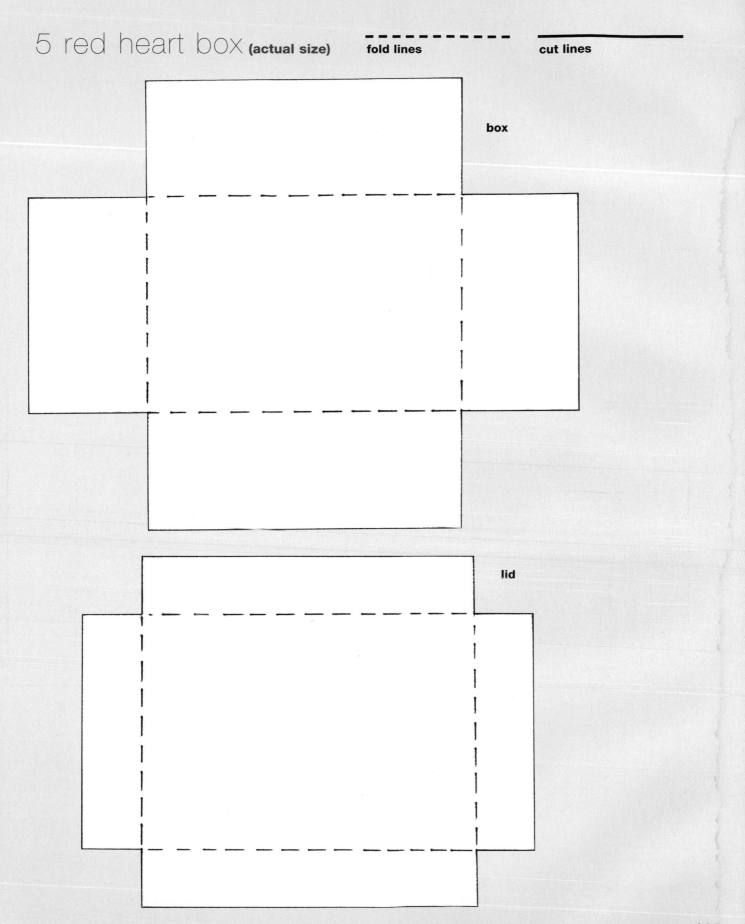

box

lid

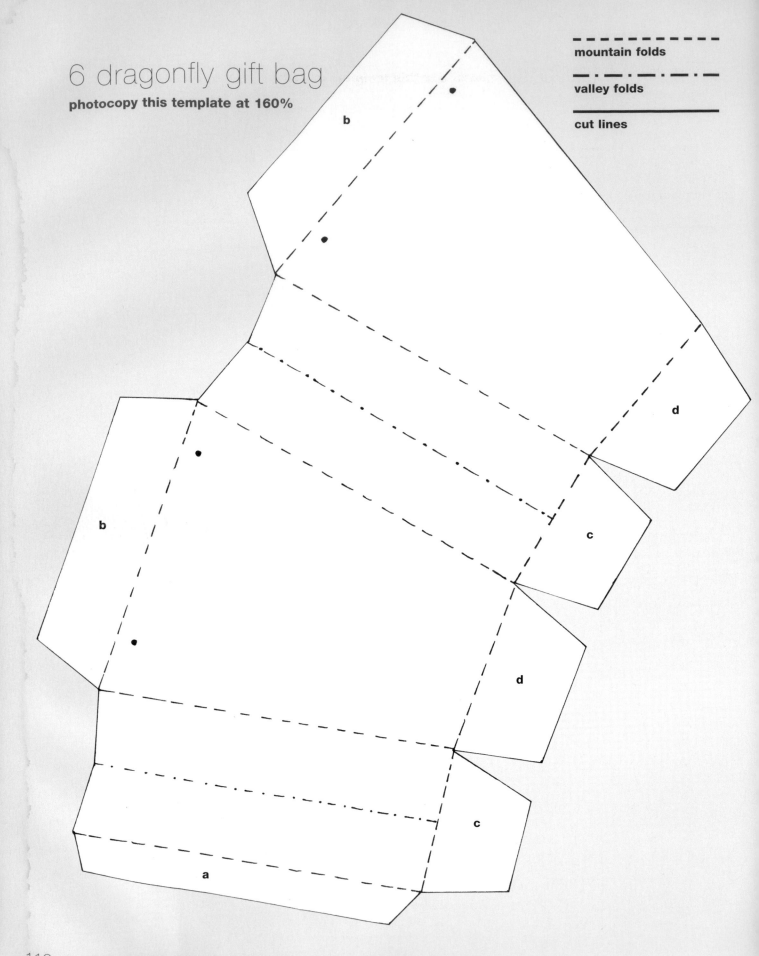

6 dragonfly gift bag
photocopy this template at 160%

mountain folds

valley folds

cut lines

b

b

d

c

d

c

a

7 pink handbag **photocopy this template at 160%**

cut lines

- - - - - -
fold lines

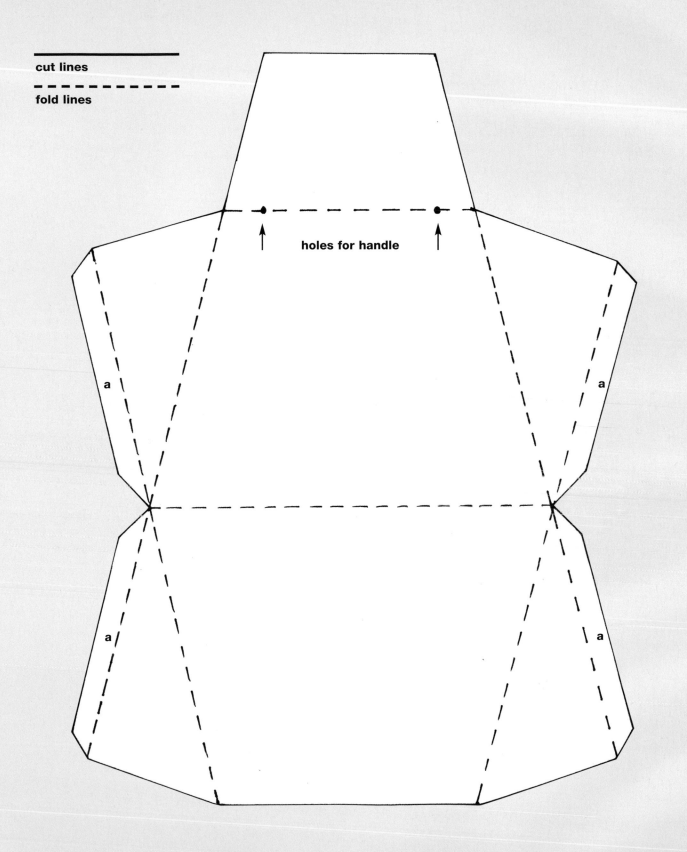

holes for handle

a

a

a

a

8 pearl
handle
bag

**photocopy this template
at 167%**

- - - - - -
mountain folds

- · - · - ·
valley folds

─────
cut lines

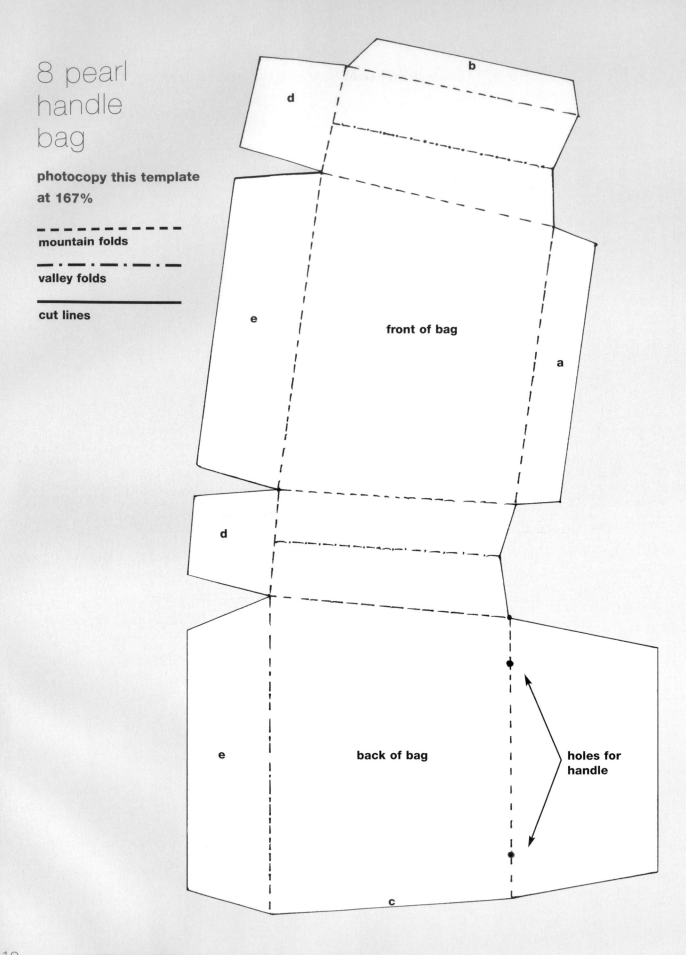

d

b

d

e

front of bag

a

d

e

back of bag

**holes for
handle**

c

9 pearl handle tag (actual size)

- - - - mountain folds

- · - · - valley folds

───── cut lines

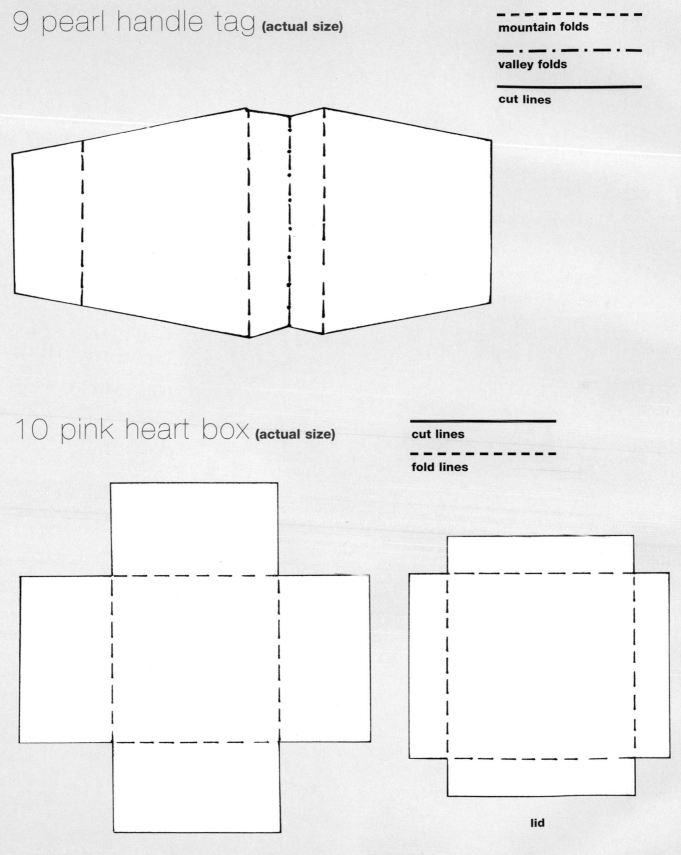

10 pink heart box (actual size)

───── cut lines

- - - - fold lines

box

lid

11 round flower box

photocopy this template at 130%

cut lines

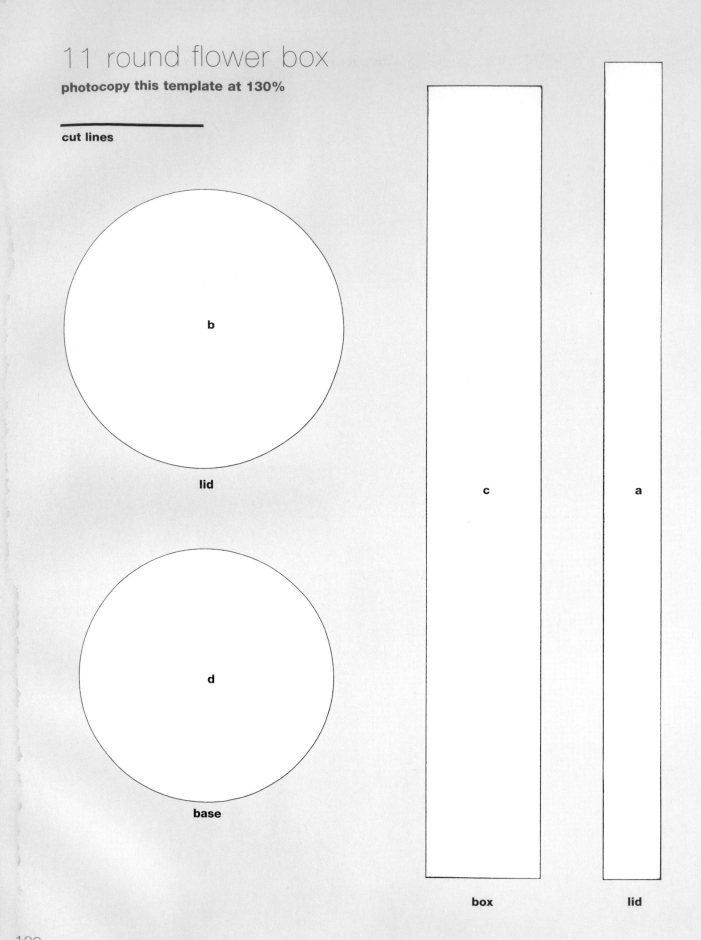

b

lid

d

base

c

box

a

lid

12 purple butterfly bag **photocopy this template at 300%**

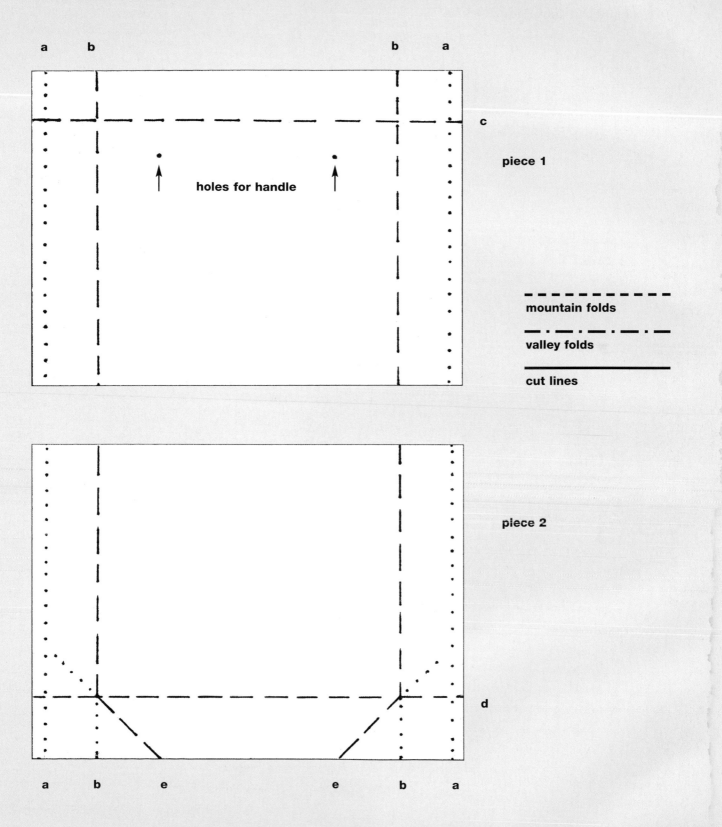

holes for handle

piece 1

- - - - - - -
mountain folds

— · — · — ·
valley folds

————————
cut lines

piece 2

13 silver box

photocopy this template at 217%

cut lines

fold lines

lid

base

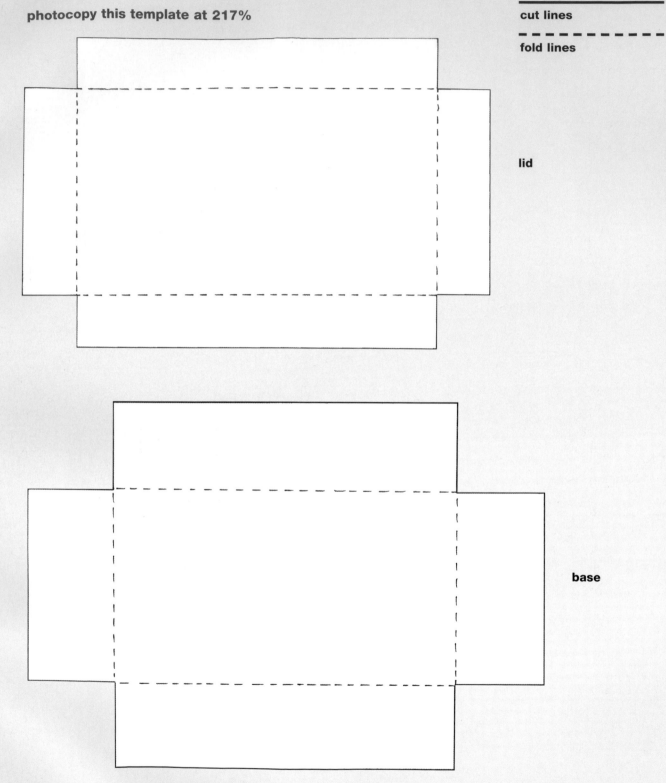

14 pink leaf bag **photocopy this template at 200%**

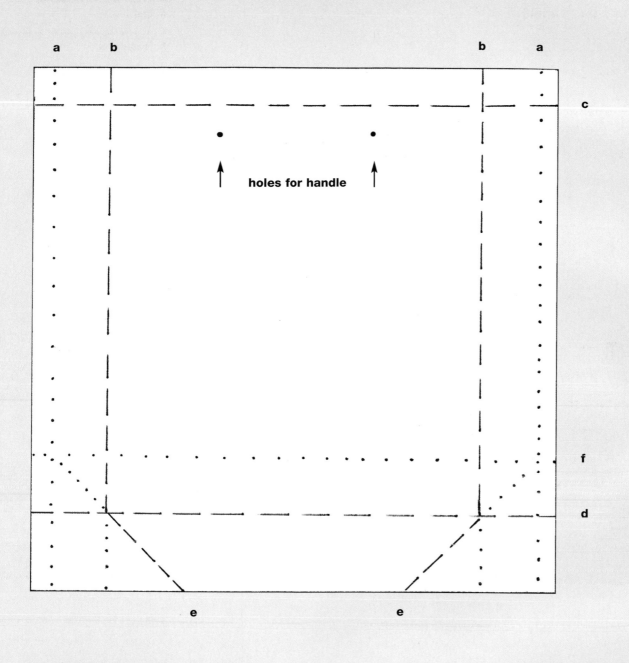

a　　b　　　　　　　　　　　　　　　　　b　　a

holes for handle

c

f

d

e　　　　　　　　e

- - - - - - - -
mountain folds

....
valley folds

────────
cut lines

15 pink feather box

photocopy this template at 150%

cut lines

- - - - - -

fold lines

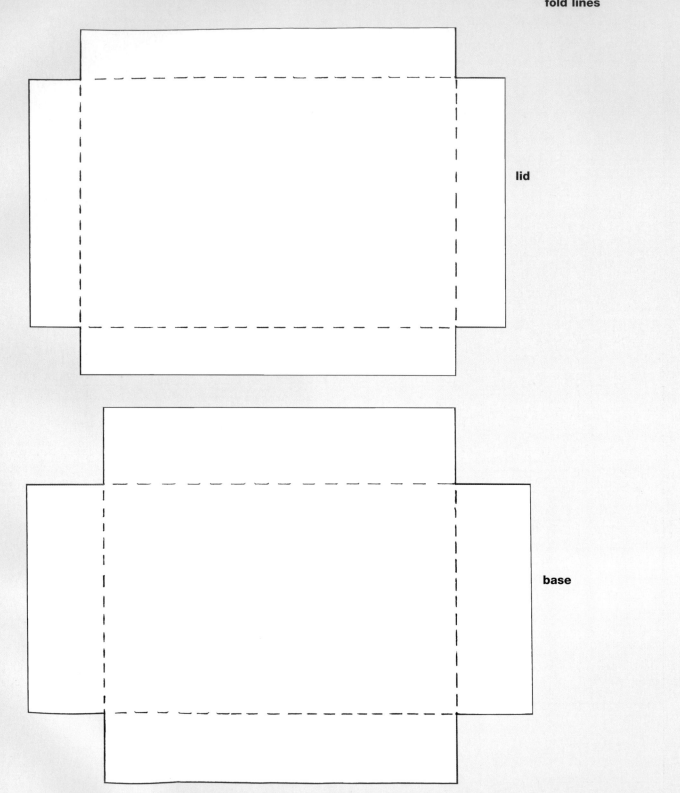

lid

base

16 pink gingham box cover **photocopy this template at 184%**

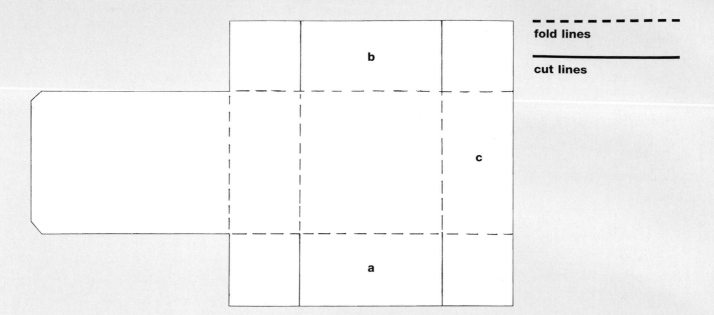

fold lines

cut lines

b

c

a

17 pin bag **photocopy this template at 220%**

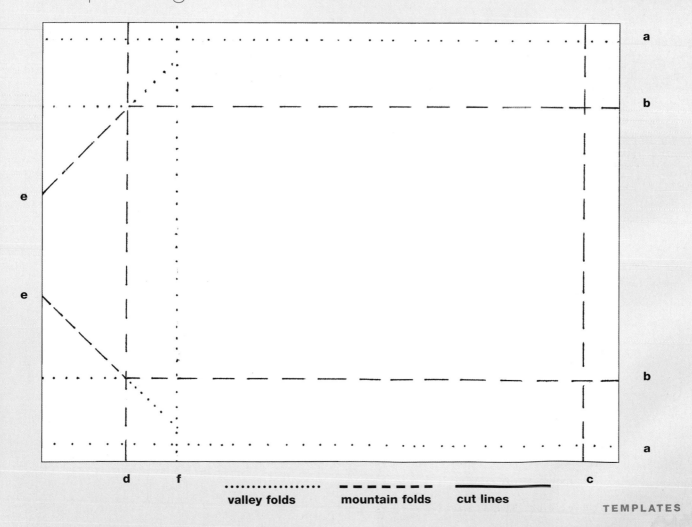

a

b

e

e

b

a

d   f

valley folds   **mountain folds**   **cut lines**

c

mail order suppliers

UK

USA

Artycrafty
9 Church Street
Godalming
Surrey
GU7 1EQ
www.artycrafty.com

Craftee
98 Brookfield Walk
Clevedon
Somerset
BS21 6YJ
www.craftee.co.uk

Craft Creations
Ingersoll House
Delamare Road
Cheshunt
Hertfordshire
EN8 9HD
www.craftcreations.com

Fred Aldous
37 Lever Street
Manchester
M1 1LW
www.fredaldous.co.uk

Hobbicraft
40 Woodhouse Lane
Merrion Centre
Leeds
LS2 8LX
www.hobbicraft.co.uk

Hobbycraft
HobbyCraft Group Limited
7 Enterprise Way
Aviation Park
Bournemouth International Airport
Dorset
BH23 6HG
www.hobbycraft.co.uk

Impress Cards
Slough Farm
Westhall
Halesworth
Suffolk
IP19 8RN
www.impress-cards.co.uk

Lakeland Limited
Alexandra Buildings
Windermere
Cumbria
LA23 1BQ
www.lakelandlimited.co.uk

The Craft Barn
9 East Grinstead Road
Lingfield
Surrey
RH7 6EP
www.craftbarn.co.uk

Crafts Etc!
7717 SW 44th Street
Oklahoma City
OK 73179
www.craftsetc.com

Craft King
12750 W. Capitol Dr.
Brookfield
WI 53005
www.craftking.com

index

Guild of Master Craftsman Publications,
Castle Place, 166 High Street, Lewes,
East Sussex BN7 1XU, United Kingdom
Tel: 01273 488005 Fax: 01273 402866
Website: www.thegmcgroup.com

Contact us for a complete catalogue, or visit our website.
Orders by credit card are accepted.